A SHORTER COMMENTARY ON GENESIS

By
LEON J. WOOD

Wipf and Stock Publishers
150 West Broadway • Eugene OR 97401
1998

A Shorter Commentary on Genesis

By Wood, Leon J.

ISBN: 1-57910-140-2

Printed by *Wipf and Stock Publishers* *1998*
150 West Broadway • Eugene OR 97401

Previously Published by The Zondervan Corporation, 1975.

Table of Contents

Special Foreword

This volume is one in a series of Dr. Leon J. Wood's works of scholarship now being made available through Wipf and Stock Publishers by arrangement with Dr. Wood's family.

It is the family's hope and prayer that this partnership will continue to make available our father's work to students of the Bible and to the Church.

The Family of Dr. Leon J. Wood, 1998

Preface

The Book of Genesis is possibly the most important book in the Bible. It tells of the beginning of all things and is therefore basic to truths set forth in later books. Every Christian should spend time in studying it and fixing its message in his or her mind and heart.

This small volume is intended to aid the Bible student in doing this. It is not a substitute for the Bible itself, but only a help and guide as one reads the Genesis account for himself. It is not intended either to be a detailed or a technical commentary for the advanced Bible student. In simple terms it relates the stories of the book together, explains portions that are more difficult to understand, and shows how archaeological research has provided considerable information as background for numerous portions.

Here are some suggested helps for using the study guide.

1. Before beginning a time of study, ask the Holy Spirit to give you understanding.

2. Read the biblical story before reading the corresponding chapter in this book.

3. Come to your study time with expectancy. Genesis is interesting, relevant, and exciting. Be mentally alert to all that is there to learn.

4. Plan to give adequate time to your study. Think through the thoughts of the chapter and fix them in your mind. When you believe you have mastered the content of a chapter, tell the thoughts to yourself (or someone else). Afterward, check both the story in the Bible and the comments in this book to see if you have left anything out.

5. Look for practical applications of the truths to your own life. Have an open heart to respond to these applications.

6. You will find significant help in your study if you read the articles in a Bible dictionary or encyclopedia as indicated at the close of the chapters of the book. Questions also are placed there to help you in your study.

Introduction

A. Name

The Book of Genesis is named in the Hebrew Bible after the first word of the book, *bereshith,* meaning "in beginning." It was customary for the Hebrew people to name their books by the first word they contained. The name "Genesis" is from the Greek word, *geneseos,* and was taken from the Septuagint (Greek) translation of Genesis 2:4a, "This is the book of the *geneseos* of heaven and earth." The word *geneseos* means "origin, source, generation." Actually the Septuagint uses *geneseos* eleven times in the book, each time rendered in our English versions as "generation." (Besides 2:4a, see 5:1; 6:9; 10:1; 11:10, 27; 25:12, 19; 36:1, 9; 37:2.) Some expositors even divide the book in accordance with these times of "beginning" or "generation." Because of both names, *bereshith* and *geneseos,* the book is well called "the book of beginnings."

B. The "beginnings" in Genesis

The appropriateness of the term "beginnings" for Genesis is seen in the record it gives of the various starting points of all that exists. Four of these "beginnings" call for special notice because of their importance to the Christian faith.

First is the beginning of the world by creation. This beginning is basic for, apart from creation, there would be no need for the Bible at all. Second is the beginning of sin. It is significant that the story of man's fall into sin comes immediately after the story of creation. Had sin not entered the created world, there would have been no need for any of the Bible following this story. The theme of the Bible is the redemption of man from this sin and its consequences.

Third is the beginning of salvation. As soon as man fell and became deserving of eternal death, God inaugurated His plan of salvation for man. This is made clear by His immediate statement to Adam and Eve that He would "put enmity between" Satan and mankind, and that though Satan would "bruise" the "heel" of the "Seed" of man (meaning basically Christ), this "Seed" would "bruise" the "head" of Satan. Fourth is the beginning of God's special people, Israel, called through Abraham. Until Abraham, God had worked generally with mankind, but, because of man's persistence in sin, God selected a special people for Himself, constituting Abraham the progenitor. Through this people, God could and did bring to existence both the written Word (Bible) and the living Word (Christ). In this way the gospel provision was made for a lost world, and God's message of salvation could go forth to all mankind once again.

C. The accuracy of Genesis

1. *Regarding the first eleven chapters*

Liberal scholars have long disclaimed the accuracy of much that the Bible contains and especially the beginning chapters of Genesis. It is thought that these chapters reflect only legendary folklore concerning the origin of the world. This viewpoint is unacceptable to all who believe in the supernatural inspiration of the Scriptures. All of the Bible was divinely inspired through human authors, and this includes these opening chapters. They are free from all inaccuracy and error. They reflect the history of earth's earliest days in a brief but literal manner, and they are to be studied and understood in the same way as any other portion of the Bible.

a. *The matter of creation vs. evolution.* One of the principal reasons for the denial of the literal accuracy of these chapters is that the chapters do not reflect an evolutionary beginning for man and his world. Evolutionists believe that the present world is the product of change, as less complicated forms of existence assumed more complex forms. Some evolutionists, who call themselves theistic evolutionists, believe that this process was superintended by God, but naturalistic evolutionists see it as the product of pure chance, energized by a force somehow inherent in the process itself. Both forms of evolution are at variance with the Genesis record.

The Genesis record says that God created the several "kinds" of living forms as such, meaning that they did not evolve from other forms. There has been development within these respective "kinds" since creation (various types of cows, horses, dogs, etc.), but the "kinds" themselves did not develop nor did they cross to make new "kinds." Again, man was created fully man, both body and soul, and did not evolve from an animal stage. Some theistic evolutionists depart from a thoroughgoing theistic evolution and say that man's soul came by direct creation from God, but still believe that his body came by the evolutionary process. The scriptural record, however, will not allow this position, for Genesis 2:7 states that God made man's body of the "dust of the ground," and then breathed into that body the "breath of life." Any fair understanding of the verse requires an immediate creation of the body as well as the soul. Besides this, woman was made after man, with both her body and soul being fashioned directly by God (Gen. 2:21-25).

b. *Truths from these chapters are basic to theology.* We find certain truths in the early chapters of Genesis which are basic in importance to the teaching of the remainder of the Bible. For instance, there is the truth of the unity of the human race. This tenet is essential to the doctrine of the imputation of sin, because all men are sinners due to having descended from one set of parents. All fell in the one man, Adam. The theory of evolution assumes that man could have evolved at various places in the world and finds no need to think of all men having developed from the same set of parents. Again, the fact of universal sin is based on the historical act of this first man in eating forbidden fruit in the Garden of Eden. Still again, the doctrine of the two representative heads, Adam and Christ (Rom. 5:12-21), makes sense only if Adam truly fell into sin just as the story presents the matter in Genesis.

2. *Regarding chapters 12 to 50*

For many years, scholars of the critical school denied the accuracy of the remaining chapters of Genesis almost as completely as that of the first eleven. They thought that these too were the result of legend and folklore. The names given to the patriarchs (Abraham, Isaac, Jacob, Joseph, etc.) were thought at best to be names of tribal groups, who may or may not have moved about somewhat in the manner depicted for the patriarchs. Some scholars spoke of the stories regarding the patriarchs as reflecting only early Canaanite tales, which later Israelite writers took over and attributed to their imagined ancestors.

This manner of thinking is not expressed often today, however, because archaelological discoveries have repeatedly given support to the accuracy of the Genesis record. A few examples of such discoveries can be noted here, and more will be introduced in the discussion of the Genesis text which follows.

One example concerns names found in Genesis. Similar names have been discovered dating to the time of the patriarchs. For instance, the name "Abraham" has been found in Babylonian texts of the sixteenth century in the form *Abamram,* and in other forms at Mari. Then there are customs, strange to us today, which are reflected in the Genesis account, and archaeology has shown that they were normal for that early day. An illustration concerns the occasion when Abram was worried that his servant, Eliezer, would be his heir instead of a son of his own (Gen. 15:1-4). The Genesis record implies that such heirship was normal when no natural son existed. Texts found at the ancient city of Nuzi show that this was indeed the case. They indicate that childless parents could adopt a servant as a son, who would then serve them for their lifetime, and that he would be their heir unless a natural son should be born.

Because of discoveries like these, W. F. Albright states, "So many corroborations of details have been discovered in recent years that most competent scholars have given up the old critical theory according to which the stories of the Patriarchs are mostly retrojections from the time of the Dual Monarchy (9th-8th centuries B.C.).[1]

D. Authorship

Probably no area of Old Testament study has given rise to greater controversy between conservative and liberal scholars than that of the authorship of the Pentateuch. Since the late eighteenth century, liberal scholars have contended Moses did not write it, but that it was written by numerous persons living many centuries later. Conservative scholars, however, taking the Bible as its own proper witness, continue to maintain that Moses was the author. Space does not permit the matter to be argued here, except to say that Jesus Himself gave clear witness to the fact. He did this in various ways, but at no time more clearly than when he equated the Torah (Pentateuch) division of the Hebrew Bible with Moses, saying, "Which were written in the law of Moses, and in the prophets, and in the psalms" (Luke 24:44; cf. 24:27; 16:31; Acts 26:22; 28:23). If Christ equated the Torah division with Moses, and Genesis was

---

[1] *From the Stone Age to Christianity,* 2nd ed. (New York: Doubleday, 1957), p. 183.

considered a part of the Torah division, then Jesus clearly ascribed Mosaic authorship to Genesis. Because He did, and because numerous other arguments could be cited to the same conclusion, without any other author being assigned to Genesis in any scriptural reference, one may be sure that Moses was the person God used to pen its pages.

This does not necessarily mean that Moses did not use some earlier materials in his writing. It is possible, for instance, that God revealed such items as the story of creation and the story of man's fall already to Abraham, who could have recorded them then under inspiration. It is altogether likely that Abraham could write, for he came from Ur of the Chaldees in a day when the city was the center of Sumerian culture. Such materials could be expected to have been preserved under God's special care and made available to Moses to use in recording the full book in his time.

The Book of Genesis divides itself into two main parts: Part 1, The Early History of Mankind (chaps. 1-11); Part 2, The History of the Patriarchs (chap. 12-50). These parts divide themselves logically into several subdivisions, and the chapter divisions of this book observe these subdivisions.

Part 1: The Early History of Mankind

Chapter 1: The Creation of the Universe

- A. The initial creation (1:1,2)
  1. Simplicity of the statement
  2. The original state of creation
- B. The six days of creation (1:3-31)
  1. The first day (1:3-5)
  2. The second day (1:6-8)
  3. The third day (1:14-19)
  4. The fourth day (1:14-19)
  5. The fifth day (1:20-23)
  6. The sixth day (1:24-31)
- C. The seventh day of rest (2:1-3)

Chapter 2: The Fall of Man

- A. The preparatory portion of the story (2:4-25)
  1. The general setting (2:4-6)

2. The creation of man (2:7)
3. The Garden of Eden (2:8-15)
4. The prohibition (2:16, 17)
5. The creation of woman

B. The story of the fall proper (3:1-24)
1. Eve and Adam eat of the tree (3:1-7)
2. God seeks out fallen man (3:8-13)
3. Pronouncement of curses (3:14-19)
4. Final events (3:20-24)

Chapter 3: A Great Increase in Sin

A. Cain murders his brother Abel (4:1-15)
1. The two sons and their respective sacrifices (4:1-5)
2. The anger of Cain (4:6, 7)
3. The murder of Abel (4:8-15)

B. The descendants of Cain (4:16-24)

C. The descendants of Seth (4:25-5:32)
1. Introduction of this godly line (4:25, 26)
2. The genealogy of Seth (5:1-32)

D. Rapid development of sin (6:1-7)

Chapter 4: The Flood

A. Instruction to Noah (6:8-7:9)
1. Preliminary matters (6:8-13)
2. Instructions regarding the ark (6:14-7:4)
3. Instructions carried out (7:5-9)

B. The Flood (7:10-8:14)
1. The Flood proper (7:10-23)
2. The duration of the Flood (7:24-8:14)

C. Noah leaves the ark (8:15-22)

D. Events immediately following the Flood (9:1-29)
1. Commands given (9:1-7)
2. A promise given (9:8-17)
3. Noah's sin followed by a curse and blessings (9:20-27)
4. Noah's death (9:28, 29)

Chapter 5: History After the Flood

A. The table of nations (10:1-32)
   1. The descendants of Japheth (10:1-5)
   2. The descendants of Ham (10:6-20)
   3. The descendants of Shem (10:21-31)

B. The tower of Babel (11:1-9)
   1. The building of the tower (11:1-4)
   2. The judgment of God (11:5-9)

C. The genealogy of Shem to Abraham (11:10-26)

D. The family of Terah (11:27-32)

Part 2: The History of the Patriarchs

Chapter 6: Abraham (I)

A. Abraham's arrival in Canaan (12:1-20)
   1. Renewed call in Harran (12:1-9)
   2. Journey to Egypt (12:10-20)

B. Return to Canaan (13:1-8)
   1. Return to Bethel (13:1-4)
   2. Prosperity a problem (13:5-13)
   3. Promise to Abraham (13:14-18)

C. Kings from the east (14:1-24)
   1. Lot captured in the defeat of Sodom (14:1-13)
   2. Rescue of Lot by Abraham (14:14-17)
   3. Meeting with Melchizedek and the king of Sodom (14:18-24)

D. The covenant restated through a vision (15:1-21)
   1. Abraham's concern (15:1-3)
   2. God's initial response (15:4-7)
   3. God's confirming sign (15:8-17)
   4. The extent of the promise (15:18-21)

E. The birth of Ishmael (16:1-16)
   1. A wrong suggestion (16:1-3)
   2. Resulting trouble (16:4-6)
   3. Hagar is met by the Angel of the Lord (16:7-12)
   4. Response of Hagar (16:13-16)

Chapter 7: Abraham (II)

A. Further reassurance of the promises (17:1-27)
  1. The promises stated (17:1-8)
  2. An obligation assigned (17:9-14)
  3. The particular promise of a son (17:15-22)
  4. Obedience rendered (17:23-27)

B. Abraham and the Angel of the Lord (18:1-33)
  1. The visit of three angels (18:1-16)
  2. The revelation concerning Sodom (18:17-22)
  3. Abraham intercedes for Sodom (18:23-33)

C. The destruction of Sodom (19:1-38)
  1. Lot is rescued by the angels (19:1-23)
  2. The destruction of Sodom (19:24-29)
  3. Lot and his two daughters (19:30-38)

D. Abraham's sin at Gerar (20:1-18)
  1. Abraham's falsehood repeated (20:1, 2)
  2. God warns Abimelech (20:3-7)
  3. Abimelech confronts Abraham (20:8-13)
  4. Abimelech's generosity toward Abraham (20:14-18)

Chapter 8: Abraham (III)

A. Birth of Isaac (21:1-34)
  1. The birth proper (21:1-8)
  2. Conflict with Ishmael (21:9-21)
  3. An interlude with Abimelech (21:22-34)

B. The offering of Isaac (22:1-24)
  1. God's directive (22:1, 2)
  2. Abraham's obedience (22:3-10)
  3. God's substitionary provision (22:11-14)
  4. The promises again confirmed (22:15-19)
  5. The family of Nahor (22:20-24)

C. Death and burial of Sarah (23:1-20)
  1. Sarah's age (23:1, 2)
  2. The purchase of the cave of Machpelah (23:3-18)
  3. Burial of Sarah (23:19, 20)

D. A Bride for Isaac (24:1-67)
   1. Abraham sends his servant to procure a bride (24:1-9)
   2. The servant finds Rebekah (24:10-27)
   3. The servant and Rebekah's family (24:28-61)
   4. The meeting with Isaac (24:61-67)

E. The last days of Abraham (25:1-18)
   1. Marriage to Keturah (25:1-6)
   2. The death of Abraham (25:7-11)
   3. The descendants of Ishmael (25:12-18)

Chapter 9: Isaac

A. The sons, Jacob and Esau (25:19-34)
   1. Their birth (25:19-26)
   2. Esau sells his birthright to Jacob (25:27-34)

B. Isaac and Abimelech (26:1-33)
   1. God appears to Isaac (26:1-5)
   2. Isaac's falsehood regarding Rebekah (26:6-15)
   3. A dispute over wells of water (26:16-33)

C. Esau's marriages (26:34, 35)

Chapter 10: Jacob (I)

A. The blessing by Isaac (27:1-46)
   1. The decision of Isaac to bless Esau (27:1-5)
   2. Rebekah and Jacob plot to deceive Isaac (27:6-17)
   3. The blessing bestowed on Jacob (27:18-29)
   4. The remorse of Esau (27:30-41)
   5. The reaction of Rebekah (27:42-46)

B. Jacob's journey to Haran (28:1-22)
   1. The departure (28:1-5)
   2. An interlude regarding Esau (28:6-9)
   3. Jacob's dream of the ladder to heaven (28:10-22)

C. Jacob's marriage to Leah and Rachel (29:1-30)
   1. Jacob's meeting with Rachel (29:1-12)
   2. The double marriage (29:13-30)

D. The birth of Jacob's sons (29:31-30:24)

E. Jacob's wages during six additional years (30:25-43)
   1. The wage agreement (30:25-36)
   2. Jacob becomes wealthy (30:37-43)

Chapter 11: Jacob (II)

A. Jacob leaves for Canaan (31:1-55)
   1. The decision to leave (31:1-16)
   2. The secret departure (31:17-21)
   3. Pursued by Laban (31:22-55)

B. Jacob's encounter with Esau (32:1-33:15)
   1. Met by angels of God (32:1, 2)
   2. Preparation to meet Esau (32:3-23)
   3. Wrestling with the Angel of the Lord (32:24-32)
   4. The meeting with Esau (33:1-15)

C. Back in Canaan (33:16-35:29)
   1. Jacob stops at Shechem (33:16-20)
   2. A sad episode with the Shechemites (34:1-31)
   3. Another experience at Bethel (35:1-15)
   4. Rachel dies in childbirth (35:16-26)
   5. Death of Isaac (35:27-29)

D. Esau's descendants and Edom (36:1-43)
   1. Descendants of Esau (36:1-19)
   2. Original inhabitants of Seir (36:20-30)
   3. Kings of Edom (36:31-39)
   4. Tribal princes from Esau (36:40-43)

Chapter 12: Joseph (I)

A. Joseph and his brothers (37:1-36)
   1. Joseph's unpopular position in his home (37:1-4)
   2. Joseph's unpopular dreams (37:5-11)
   3. The plot of the brothers against Joseph (37:12-27)
   4. Joseph sold into Egypt (37:28-36)

B. Judah and Tamar (38:1-30)
   1. Judah marries the daughter of a Canaanite, Shuah (38:1-10)
   2. Judah and his daughter-in-law Tamar (38:11-26)
   3. Birth of twins, Pharez and Zerah (38:27-30)

C. Joseph and Potiphar's wife (39:1-23)
   1. Joseph tempted by Potiphar's wife (39:1-13)
   2. Joseph imprisoned (39:14-23)

D. Interpreting the dreams of the butler and baker (40:1-23)
   1. Pharaoh's butler and baker have dreams (40:1-8)
   2. The butler's dream (40:9-15)
   3. The baker's dream (40:16-19)
   4. The result (40:20-23)

Chapter 13: Joseph (II)

A. A dream of Pharaoh results in Joseph's promotion (41:1-57)
   1. Pharoah's double dream (41:1-8)
   2. The butler remembers (41:9-13)
   3. Joseph interprets Pharaoh's dream (41:14-32)
   4. Joseph's advice and promotion (41:33-46)
   5. Joseph's administration (41:47-57)

B. Joseph's brothers come to Egypt (42:1-38)
   1. The brothers meet Joseph (42:1-28)
   2. Report to Jacob (42:29-38)

C. A second visit of the brothers (43:1-45:18)
   1. Preparations for departure (43:1-14)
   2. The brothers stand before Joseph again (43:15-34)
   3. The brothers start home (44:1-13)
   4. The intercession of Judah before Joseph (44:14-34)
   5. Joseph reveals himself to his brothers (45:1-15)
   6. Jacob is told the good news (45:16-28)

Chapter 14: Joseph (III)

A. Jacob travels to Egypt (46:1-34)
   1. Reassurance from God (46:1-4)
   2. The journey to Egypt (46:5-27)
   3. Arrival in Egypt (46:28-34)

B. Jacob's family in Egypt (47:1-31)
   1. Jacob meets Pharaoh (47:1-12)
   2. Joseph's work in overseeing Egypt (47:13-26)
   3. Jacob's last days (47:27-31)

C. Jacob blesses the sons of Joseph (48:1-22)

1. Joseph brings his sons before Jacob (48:1-11)
2. The blessing bestowed (48:12-22)

D. Jacob blesses his own sons (49:1-33)

1. Reuben (49:3, 4)
2. Simeon and Levi (49:5-7)
3. Judah (49:8-12)
4. Zebulun (49:13)
5. Issachar (49:14, 15)
6. Dan (49:16-18)
7. Gad (49:19)
8. Asher (49:20)
9. Naphtali (49:21)
10. Joseph (49:22-26)
11. Benjamin (49:27)
12. Jacob's directive regarding his burial (49:29-33)

E. Burial of Jacob and death of Joseph (50:1-26)

1. Burial of Jacob (50:1-14)
2. Joseph's brothers now fear him (50:15-21)
3. Joseph's last days (50:22-26)

PART ONE: THE EARLY HISTORY OF MANKIND

Chapter 1

The Creation of the Universe

(Genesis 1:1 — 2:3)

The Bible begins where it must — with creation. Before creation, God alone existed. He is eternal, without beginning or ending. But God chose to create something other than Himself, which means out of no preexisting substance; this "something" was the universe, which includes the planet earth on which man resides. Apart from this creation man would have no existence and there would be no need for a Bible.

A. The initial creation (Gen. 1:1, 2)

1. *Simplicity of the statement*

While finite man in his limited reasoning has thought and written much on how the world came to being, God stated the matter in the simplest of terms: "In the beginning God created the heaven and the earth." God, not blind chance, is responsible for it, and He created it from no prior substance. He provided the plan and He energized the act, but the substance came *ex nihilo,* from nothing. Because this fact is contrary to man's daily experience, it is rejected as impossible by many people, and some explanation involving evolution is attempted as a substitute. Still the basic problem of the origin of the first substance faces any evolutionist, and his only answer, if he rejects creationism, is to say that substance itself must somehow be eternal. But no substance has the properties of eternality, as does God. The phrase "heaven and earth" includes all the universe, not only earth, where man resides, but all heavenly bodies as well.

2. *The original state of creation*

For some reason God did not choose to bring the initial creation to a completed state. Verse 2 says that it was "without form, and void," with darkness everywhere. Some believe that this condition resulted from a judgment of God, but at least this verse gives no evidence of this. The Hebrew word for "was" can be translated "became," but it is the normal word for "was" all the way through the Old Testament.

That the Spirit of God began to move "upon the face of the waters" indicates that the Third Person of the Godhead began to bring order out of this "waste and void" condition. God the Father planned creation. God the Son effected creation (John 1:3; Col. 1:16), and God the Holy Spirit brought creation to completion. Similarly, God the Father planned man's salvation (recreation), God the Son effected the plan (incarnation and death), and God the Holy Spirit applies the benefit to sinners, thus bringing the plan to completion once again.

B. The six days of creation (Gen. 1:3-31)

The work of the Holy Spirit in bringing creation to completion was done in six days. The length of these days — whether twenty-four hours or longer periods of time — has been cause for much discussion. Whatever the length, the important matter is that the Bible, and not scientific claims, is allowed to be the final authority. It is important also to maintain that God created immediately and instantaneously, whenever an act of creation was effected: He did not use mediate matter nor a process of time. God did not need even six days for this creation. He might have done everything in six seconds, or even instantaneously. He chose, however, to use six days.

1. *The first day (Gen. 1:3-5)*

God's first act was to dispel the darkness with the creation of light. Some believe that this means the sun was created at this time, with light filtering down through a haze of atmospheric vapor. This is possible, but is not favored by the statement concerning the fourth day when God said, "Let there be lights in the firmament of the heaven" (1:14). Light, after all, is God's creation, whether made by the medium of the sun or in some other way. God divided "the light from the darkness" in that He caused a portion of a twenty-four hour cycle to be characterized by light, calling this portion "day," and a portion by darkness, calling it "night."

The word order in verse 5, mentioning "evening" before "morning," is best explained as follows: "evening" was the closing of the first day, and "morning" the beginning of the second day. If the two together were intended to recapitulate the whole first day, one would expect the order "morning" and "evening."

2. *The second day (Gen. 1:6, 7)*

God's second act was to constitute a proper atmospheric condition for the earth. He divided the vaporous water of the atmosphere from water on the earth. Apparently before this a cloud-fog condition existed all around the earth. If plants were to live and man and animals were to see, however, this condition had to be changed. Therefore, God made the "expanse" (better translation than "firmament") to divide between clouds above and land-water below.

3. *The third day (Gen. 1:9-13)*

On the third day, a first act of God was to effect another form of separation; water from soil. It seems that before this time water and soil were mixed, so that the land surface consisted of a sort of mud, a fluid mass. God now caused the water to separate from the soil so that it was collected into streams, lakes, and seas, and the soil was allowed to dry into a solid from which plants could grow and on which animals and man could walk.

On this day, also, God provided for the existence of plant life. The earth, now made appropriately solid, was commanded to "bring forth" grass and fruit trees, all after their kind," and this occurred. It may be objected that nothing is said here about creation as such. The thought of verses 11 and 12 seems to be that God at this time created the process by which the earth produces plants. This means that He must either have created the seed, which the earth then generated into plants, or the full grown plants that produced the seed, which then the earth made produce more plants. Either way, a work of creation was required. That "God saw that it was good" means that He was pleased with what was produced.

4. *The fourth day (Gen. 1:14-19)*

It should be noticed that the second set of three days, which begins here with the fourth day, has a definite correspondence to the first set. On this fourth day, the light bearers of the heavens were formed. This corresponds to the light which was created on the first day. The purpose of the light bearers is assigned in verse 14: to establish time divisions: days, seasons, and years. Verse 16 stresses formation of the sun and moon, for these are important to the earth where man dwells, and they play their respective roles as light bearers in the day and in the night (v. 18).

5. *The fifth day (Gen. 1:20-23)*

The fifth day corresponds with the second day in that birds of the air were created on the fifth, and it was on the second day that the proper atmosphere for them was formed. In addition, on this same fifth day sea life was formed, and in this respect a correspondence to the third day is seen, for then the streams, lakes, and seas were made. It should be noticed that both the birds and the sea creatures were also made after their "kind." Each "kind" was made unique and distinct from every other. The "kinds" did not evolve from a common ancestor, as evolutionists claim. With this form of life existence, mating is first involved, and accordingly God bids both birds and sea life to multiply in number (v. 22).

6. *The sixth day (Gen. 1:24-31)*

The sixth day is the busy day of creation, for God created much more on that day than on any other day. A correspondence with the third day is seen in that both animals and man were created to inhabit the solid earth formed on the third day. Animals constituted the first creation of this day, made again "after their kind" (vv. 24, 25).

Then man, the apex of God's creative work, was created on this sixth day. He was made in the "image" of God. That God saw this to be uniquely important is made clear by the stress on the thought in two verses (vv. 26, 27). Man was made after God's own pattern, only on a finite level. This means that he was made a personality, with the power of self-consciousness and self-determination. It means, further, that he was made in "knowledge," "righteousness," and "holiness" (Eph. 4:24; Col. 3:10). As a person, then, created fresh from the hand of God, he possessed "knowledge," walked in "righteousness," and had a "holy" character. It should be observed, further, in respect to God's creative work with man, that a reference to the trinity of God is implied in the language used. The first plural pronoun is significantly employed in respect to God, as God says, "Let *us* make man in *our* image."

Man was bidden not only to multiply in number, as were the birds and sea life, but also to have dominion over all lower creation (v. 28). As a first demonstration of this superiority of man, he was commanded to name all the animals (2:18, 19). Evolutionists think of man in his early stage as little above the brute level, lacking in intelligence. But Adam displayed the highest intelligence in giving names to animals, no doubt seeking names that suited each "kind." This must have been a sizeable task, but it was still accomplished on the sixth day, because woman was formed after he was finished. And Genesis 1:26, 27 makes clear that man, as both male and female, was created on the sixth day.

Then there was this task of making woman. Adam was put into a deep sleep as God took a "rib" (Hebrew says merely, "one from his sides") and from it made woman.

In verses 28 and 29, the food supply of both man and animals is indicated: the herbs and trees that had been created prior to both. The last statement is that God saw everything that He had made as "very good." It had come from the hand of God and, therefore, could only be good.

C. The seventh day of rest (Gen. 2:1-3)

Two points are made regarding the seventh day. First, God "ended his work" and "rested." The word for "ended" means to "complete, finish," and that for "rested" means to "cease from work." So, then, God ended His creative activity and ceased to perform it. This "ceasing" is called "resting" in Exodus 20:11, a term close in thought. Hebrews 4:9, 10 seems to imply that God's rest from this creative labor still continues.

The second point is that, accordingly, God "blessed the seventh day and sanctified it" (v. 3). That is, He set it apart as a special day for Himself. Because He did, it became the pattern for the later commandment to man that man observe every seventh day in his work-week, ceasing then from his ordinary labor (Exod. 20:8-11).

For Further Study

1. In a Bible dictionary or encyclopedia (see bibliography) read articles on: creation, light, plants, animals, man.
2. What parallel do you see between God's creation of the world and His recreation of man at the time of his salvation?
3. At what points in the creation story do the main aspects appear in which the Bible shows itself opposed to the theory of evolution?
4. Do you believe theistic evolution is really any nearer the truth of the Bible than thorough naturalistic evolution? Explain.
5. Memorize the creative acts of God on each of the six days.

Chapter 2

The Fall of Man

(Genesis 2:4 — 3:24)

Sometimes Genesis 2:4-25 is called the second account of creation. The passage does speak about creation, but from a totally different point of view than chapter 1. It is really the beginning of the "fall" story, giving additional details regarding creation which are necessary for understanding the story of Adam and Eve and the forbidden fruit. That is the reason for the new type of beginning with 2:4, where one reads, "These are the generations of the heavens and of the earth." It also is the reason for the different manner in which the facts of creation are set forth.

It is the reason, further, for the marked change in name for God used in this chapter. The name for God employed in 1:1-2:3 is "Elohim" (the name of God connoting His transcendent, infinite power, used thirty-five times there), while in 2:4-3:24, the name is regularly Yahweh-Elohim (Yahweh meaning the condescending, gracious God, willing to reveal to man and hear prayer, used twenty times in these chapters). The meaning of "Elohim" fits the context of 1:1-2:3, for this context concerns power in the enactment of creation. The meaning of "Yahweh," however, fits 2:4-3:24 because here God is seen coming down to walk and talk with created man in the Garden of Eden.

A. The preparatory portion of the story (Gen. 2:4-25)

1. *The general setting (Gen. 2:4-6)*

Each item mentioned in this chapter carries a preparatory significance for the story of man's fall. Verses 4-6 do this by presenting the general setting of the occasion.

Verse 4 gives an introductory statement. It provides a definite clue that a new story, from that of creation in 1:1-2:3, is starting.

It also is the first instance in Genesis of the characteristic phrase, "These are the generations of. . . ." As observed in the Introduction (p. 9), this phrase occurs eleven times in the book, usually in reference to a list of names that follow. In this first instance, however, the "generations" concerned are those of the "heavens and the earth when they were created." The thought is that the following verses present the first events involving man in his relation to the new "heavens and the earth," as they had just been formed for him by God. The word "generations" is used here in the sense of "beginnings," not "generations" of human posterity.

Verses 5 and 6 set forth the situation prior to man's creation; they show both the suitability and the need for man's existence. Verse 5 says that man was needed because the earth had to be tilled, and there was no one to do this. The portion of earth Adam was to till certainly was within the Garden of Eden.

Verse 6 speaks of a need God met so that crops would grow when man tilled the soil. This was the provision of a water supply by means of a "mist." The word for "mist" is used only here in the Old Testament, and its meaning is uncertain. It may mean a mist or vapor, as commonly translated, or it may refer to a subterranean stream. Some expositors believe that it was only the Garden of Eden that was watered in this special manner, rather than the whole earth. One may say for sure that at least the Garden of Eden was provided with water by this "mist" or "subterranean river."

2. *The creation of man (Gen. 2:7)*

With the general situation of the world set forth, the first item of importance to the discussion of the Fall is to tell of man's creation. This is done now in greater detail than in Genesis 1:26, 27. Man's body was formed from the "dust of the ground." "Dust" here refers to the various elements of the earth. Chemical analysis of man's body has shown the validity of this statement. The human body is made of earth's constituent elements. Then into the body so formed, God instilled the person of man, here called "living soul." The verse makes clear, then, that both aspects of man came directly by God's creative act: the material body and the immaterial soul.

3. *The Garden of Eden (Gen. 2:8-15)*

Now man's initial habitat, the Garden of Eden, is described. This is where the Fall would take place, and accordingly there was need to describe it. Verse 9 tells of the trees of the garden. Many were made to grow, but, of these, two were given special designations: "the tree of life," and "the tree of knowledge of good and evil." Both trees are said to have been located in the central part of the garden. It may be that God wanted them where man would encounter them frequently. It should be noted that, having so mentioned them, no further reference to them is made (apart from a prohibition regarding one in v. 17) until chapter 3. This is in keeping further with the thought that chapter 2 simply presents matters necessary to be known for the understanding of the story proper in chapter 3.

Attention is now given to a river that helped to water the garden (in addition to the "mist"). Because the Flood occurred after the time here discussed, when great changes in the earth's surface certainly took place, the description of this river and its four divisions may correspond only roughly to the river system of the region as it is known today.

The identity of two of the river divisions, however, is all but certain. The third river, here named "Hiddekel," is surely the Tigris. In fact, the Tigris is the river clearly mentioned in Daniel 10:4, where this same name "Hiddekel" is used for it. Then the fourth river is called by the same name by which it is still known today, the "Euphrates." At one time these two rivers flowed together, thus making one river, before arriving at the Persian Gulf. The other two rivers, the "Pison" and the "Gihon," cannot be identified with certainty, but evidently also flowed into the same basic river system at this early point in history.

Thus, because the two known rivers joined north of the Persian Gulf, the probable location of the Garden of Eden is ascertained. It must have been where these rivers joined, just north of the gulf. In passing it may be observed that the translation "Ethiopia" (v. 13), in respect to the river Gihon, can hardly be correct, because Ethiopia is several hundred miles from either the Tigris or the Euphrates, far southwest in Africa. The Hebrew word is *cush,* which often does mean Ethiopia (or perhaps better, Nubia, just north), but clearly does not in this instance. The area in reference is unknown.

The last notice regarding the garden is that it was there that God caused man to live and that man's task was to care for it. Man's situation as here created by God was most attractive: he lived in a thriving garden, had a fine river to enjoy, and ate the best of food.

4. *The prohibition (Gen. 2:16, 17)*

The next item of information is that God laid down a prohibition for man. He was not to eat of one of the two designated trees, "the tree of knowledge of good and evil." If he did, he would "surely die." It is noteworthy that God did not give a reason to man for this prohibition. He simply stated it, evidently desiring that man obey the directive without a reason having to be provided.

No doubt Adam came to know the reason in due time, and its nature is discernible to us from the full story and Scripture generally. It was not that the fruit was poisonous or even any different from other fruit available in the garden. It was that God was hereby laying down a test for man, to see whether he would obey a simple command of God or not. Man had been doing what God desired prior to this time, true enough, but it was done quite as a matter of course. It had not been real obedience, in which a definite choice between alternatives was made. God had entrusted man with a will, and He wanted it used properly. This means that man's will should be used to obey God by choice. But one does not choose to do one thing without choosing not to do another. Alternatives must be faced, and a selection made. In this prohibition, God gave man an alternative from which to make a selection.

5. *The creation of woman (Gen. 2:18-25)*

One more item of preparatory information still remains: the creation of woman. The story of her creation is presented by telling first of man's lack of a companion. God let man realize this by having all animal life pass before him, that he might give a name to each. As noted earlier, this must have been a challenging task, in view of the many "kinds" of animals that existed. And that man gave each "kind" more than a mere glance is indicated by the fact that he found none that was suitable to him as a companion. Each evidently was considered, rejected as an appropriate companion, and then given a name that seemed to fit its nature. Implied in this is the fact that man must have been created with the ability of speech. Just as man was created mature in body, he evidently was created also with marked maturity in extent of knowledge.

With a companion not being found, God now provided one. He put Adam to sleep and then took "one of his ribs" from which to form woman. The term "rib" is really an implied meaning from the Hebrew (cf. p. 27), but, whether the item was a rib or some other bone or even a piece of flesh from man's side, at least woman was made from a part of man. The significance is that woman was to be man's counterpart, not a fresh creation as man had been. She, being made from a part of man, was constituted subservient to him as a suitable companion and source of help.

In keeping with this purpose for woman, verse 24 gives God's statement in respect to the continuing close relationship that should exist between any man and his companion. God declared that a man and wife should cleave to one another, in an abiding relationship, even leaving their own parents to do so. A final note given, to stress further the closeness and intimacy of this first pair of parents, is that they were both naked and still felt no sense of shame in each other's presence.

B. The story of the Fall (Gen. 3:1-24)

Chapter 3 now presents the story of man's fall. The story is basic to the remainder of the Bible, for it gives the reason for God's redemptive plan with which the remainder of Scripture is concerned.

1. *Eve and Adam eat of the tree (Gen. 3:1-7)*

The story begins with the coming of "the serpent" to the woman, named Eve, to tempt her to eat of the forbidden fruit. That the one bringing this temptation was really Satan, only using the physical body of a serpent, is made clear by a comparison of the following passages: John 8:44; Romans 16:20; 2 Corinthians 11:3; 1 Timothy 2:14; Revelation 12:9; and 20:2. The reason God permitted Satan to bring the temptation was no doubt to point up the test given to man. Apart from the temptation, man might not have really considered the possibility of eating of the tree. And God wanted a true choice of obedience, if it would be that man would render obedience. Man should truly select between clear alternatives that had been genuinely considered.

Satan tempted by using the strategy of raising doubt in Eve's mind. He asked, "Yea, has God said, You shall not eat of every tree of the garden?" Satan of course knew that God had so spoken, otherwise he would not have come. He wanted the woman to think about it, however, and wonder a little if God really had said this. In coming to Eve, rather than Adam, Satan had the final design in mind of causing Adam to fall, for Adam was the representative head of the human race, not Eve. He evidently believed he could deceive Eve easier, so that she would eat and then be of help in persuading Adam to do the same (cf. 1 Tim. 2:14).

Eve's response to Satan was quite different than that of Christ years later. Christ quoted Scripture and said, "Get thee hence, Satan" (Matt. 4:10). Eve, however, answered Satan's question, thus showing willingness to listen to what he might have to say. This is always the wrong response to any source of evil. It should be summarily dismissed.

Eve answered quite well in her first reply, so far as the nature of the answer is concerned. She no doubt thought at the time that she was acting properly. Satan's next statement, however, surely should have turned her away from him, for he now deliberately lied, saying, "You shall not surely die." And then to this he added the outrageous charge that God was taking advantage of Adam and Eve by the prohibition, in that they would become wise like Himself if they ate. In this way he attempted to appear as their real friend, letting them in on the fact that God was working against them. Eve's response, of course, should have been to deny the truth of such a thought flatly and demand the serpent leave her at once.

Instead, she clearly now looked at the tree, to see if perhaps there was something about it that would fit in with the surprising words just spoken. Sufficient doubt had been implanted for her to consider the possibility that she was hearing truth from the serpent. When she looked, suddenly the tree appeared differently. She now saw in a new way that it "was good for food" (implying better food than the other trees afforded, for she had always seen it as good), "that it was pleasant to the eyes" (suddenly more attractive than ever before), and now for the first time that it was desirable "to make one wise."

In other words, she saw just what Satan wanted her to see. The craft of Satan was most persuasive with Eve, as it has been with millions of people since. How the Christian should fear him and take the advice of James 4:7: "Submit yourselves therefore to God. Resist the devil, and he will flee from you." The result was that the woman took of the fruit and ate it, directly in disobedience to God's clear command, which she had herself just repeated in her first response to the serpent.

The situation would have been bad enough if the story ended there, but verse 6 continues with one of the most serious assertions of all Scripture: "And gave also unto her husband with her; and he did eat."

Let there be no mistake; Adam was in no way doing his wife a favor by also eating. He was not showing love for her, as is sometimes said. What he should have done was remonstrate with her and then beseech God, along with her, for her forgiveness. After all, she was not the representative head of the human race; Adam was. The great harm was done when he ate, not when she ate. Adam was the main object of Satan's attack from the first, and, when Adam ate, Satan achieved his goal. When Adam thus disobeyed God's command, sin entered the human race and all his posterity fell with him.

The first action of Adam and Eve, having thus sinned, was to try and hide from God. They made coverings for their bodies from fig leaves and then hid themselves. Man in his sin does not want to be found out by God, but God always knows (Prov. 15:3).

2. *God seeks out fallen man (Gen. 2:8-13)*

God in grace soon came looking for the fallen pair. They heard Him walking in the garden and calling out to them, "Where are you?" Hearing these words, the two trembled in fear. What formerly had been a joy — just to talk with God in the garden — now became a terror. What awful things sin does to man and his relation to God.

Now followed an interchange of conversation that would be amusing, if it were not so serious. Man said that he had hid himself because he was naked, and God asked him how he knew he was naked. God thus wanted man to admit to the sin that had brought this knowledge to him. Adam admitted what he had done, but not without first seeking to place the blame on his wife; and he did this by making the point that God had given her to him, thus even placing some blame on God Himself. God then addressed Eve, and she in turn was quick to place the blame on the serpent who had "beguiled" her.

Both Adam and Eve were quick to point the finger of blame away from themselves, and all their descendants have been quick to do the same. Certainly God would have been far more pleased if both had directly admitted their guilt. He knew they were guilty; there was nothing they could say to change the knowledge He already had of what they had done. It would have helped if they had been honest enough to state the true facts openly.

3. *Pronouncement of curses (Gen. 3:14-19)*

God did not address the serpent now, or give him any chance to try to make his guilt any less. He proceeded directly to pronounce curses on all three parties, the serpent, the woman, and the man, observing that order.

Verse 14 records the curse God gave to the serpent. This creature would now move about on its belly, eating of the "dust" of the ground, as it crawled through this dust (cf. Mic. 7:17). The implication is that the serpent had before propelled itself in some other manner, with this altered manner of movement being one of degradation. Probably no animal is despised or causes fear like the serpent, even today. In this it is a fitting symbol of Satan.

Verse 15 gives the curse God pronounced on Satan. God would put "enmity" between him and the woman and between the respective posterities of both. By this statement God rectified the false alignment of friendship that Satan had sought to make. Satan had made himself out as man's friend and God as man's enemy. But here God declared that the real enmity lay between man and Satan, not between man and God. The lines of battle God thus designated, between the hosts of Satan and the followers of God, has raged since this early time and still continues. Christians are bidden to be true soldiers in God's army in the continuing struggle (see Eph. 6:12-18; 2 Tim. 2:3).

The word "seed," as used here by God, carries a twofold reference: first, to Christ as the Seed personified; and, second, to all redeemed descendants of the woman. It is in the first sense especially that the last of the verse speaks of Satan as bruising the Seed's "heel," and the Seed as then bruising Satan's "head." Satan bruised Christ in that Jesus had to die on Calvary to pay the price of man's sin, but in so doing Christ bruised Satan's head, for thereby He made redemption available for lost men and women (Heb. 2:14). This great statement by God is often called the *protevangelium,* or "first gospel." It is the first promise in the Bible that a Savior would come to defeat Satan on behalf of man.

On the woman and the man God pronounced both a curse and a blessing. In respect to the woman, the curse was to consist in the fact that her child-bearing would be "in sorrow." The blessing would be that she would be able to bear children, though only in this difficult manner. The fact that her husband would "rule over" her can hardly be thought of as the result of sin. This fact actually was pictured already in the manner by which woman was made. It was appropriate to mention the fact here, for the woman had acted contrary to this principle when she led her husband into eating the forbidden fruit.

Regarding the man, his curse was that the ground would now be cursed on account of him. For this reason, "thorns" and "thistles" would grow to hinder him in his cultivating activity, so that his work would be toilsome, bringing "the sweat" to his face. Also, he would now "return unto the ground" in death and become "dust" once again, from which he had been made. This was God's announcement that the penalty He had foretold (Gen. 2:17) had truly been applied. Man was now mortal and would die physically in due course. God said that "in the day" that he would eat he would die. This did happen spiritually. Adam lost his spiritual life immediately on sinning. He did not lose his physical life that day, for God had things for him yet to do. He did become mortal, however, subject to death. The blessing for man was that, though having to labor in difficulty, he thus would be able to "eat of" the earth (v. 17). The ground would produce for him if he was diligent in working it.

4. *Final events (Gen. 3:20-24)*

The story closes with three matters noted. The first (v. 20) is that Adam gave his wife a name: *hawah,* which has come to be pronounced "Eve." The name signifies life or life-source. Adam so named his wife because he recognized her as the "mother of all living."

The second matter (v. 21) is that God now gave Adam and Eve more permanent clothing. He made them "coats of skins." Skins were more durable than fig leaves, which the two had made for themselves. To procure the skins necessitated the death of animals; thus death was caused that man might be clothed. The oft-drawn parallel that Christ's death was necessary that man might be clothed in His righteousness may be appropriate and divinely intended.

The third matter concerns man's expulsion from the garden. He was driven from his fine place of dwelling, and a "flaming sword," apparently under the control of angelic "Cherubim," was made to protect the garden from man's possible reentry. The reason given (v. 22) was thus to keep man, now having fallen, from putting "forth his hand" and taking "also of the tree of life" and so eating and living "for ever." The thought cannot be that God thus was protecting man from some magic life-potion in the fruit of this tree, which would keep him alive eternally in his fallen state. The fruit, without question, was like any other fruit. It had been constituted as the "tree of life" only because God so designated it.

The thought is rather in the realm of symbolism. Had man passed his test, and not eaten of the tree of the knowledge of good and evil, he would have been instructed by God to eat of this second tree, as the symbol of the eternal life he had now gained for himself through obedience. But since he disobeyed God and died, it was necessary that he be kept from eating it; for the tree was intended as much a symbol should he disobey as if he had obeyed. That is, if he had obeyed, the eating of it would have symbolized the life he had gained; but because he disobeyed, his not being allowed to eat it symbolized the death he had brought on himself for the disobedience. Thus, to impress man that he had indeed died, it was necessary that he be kept from eating it.

For Further Study

1. In a Bible dictionary or encyclopedia (see bibliography) read articles on: fall of man, Satan, serpent, tree of knowledge of good and evil, tree of life, cherubim.
2. Compare the temptation experienced by Christ in the wilderness (Matt. 4:1-11; Luke 4:1-13) and the temptation here of Adam and Eve.
3. What factors contribute to making obedience of a higher kind and quality? Were these factors present in the manner of God's test for Adam and Eve?
4. Can the same act of obedience by two different Christians today carry a different qualitative value in the sight of God? Explain your answer.
5. Why do you think Satan assumed the form of a serpent when he came to tempt Eve?

Chapter 3

A Great Increase in Sin

(Genesis 4:1 — 6:7)

Man did not desist in sin, after being expelled from his paradise garden. No indication is made in respect to Adam and Eve personally, but their posterity continued in the sin the parents had started, and then became worse. This is shown first in the story of Cain and Abel and the murder of the latter by the former.

A. Cain murders his brother Abel (Gen. 4:1-15)

1. *The two sons and their respective sacrifices (Gen. 4:1-5)*

Cain and Abel were the first children of Adam and Eve. Cain became a farmer, tilling the soil, while Abel became a shepherd, keeping sheep. In time both brought an offering to God. Cain brought of his farm produce and Abel of his sheep. In some undisclosed manner, God indicated His approval and acceptance of Abel's offering, but not of Cain's. Two factors may be noted for the differing evaluation God placed on the two offerings.

The one is that Abel's offering was of the "firstlings" (the best) of his flock, while Cain offered merely "of the ground," thus not necessarily of the best. The Scriptures are clear that God always wants man to give Him of his best, not second best. The second factor is even more significant. It is that Abel's offering involved the shedding of blood, as an animal was made to die, whereas Cain's did not. There was no blood to be shed in his vegetables or fruits. It is true that no recorded revelation is given regarding blood-type sacrifices prior to this time, but it is likely that there had been, in order to account both for Abel's bringing such a sacrifice and God's approval of it in contrast to that of Cain.

2. *The anger of Cain (Gen. 4:6, 7)*

That Cain's motivation had not been right in the bringing of his offering is now shown clearly by his intense anger that it was not accepted by God. If he would have reacted differently, asking penitently why his offering had been judged improper, one would commend him for at least bringing some offering to God. In view of his anger, however, one must judge that his reason for bringing the offering had itself been improper.

God now came to Cain to ask him why he was angry. Cain did not answer the question, if, indeed, God gave him opportunity. God's interest, clearly, was to impress Cain with an important truth. If Cain was acting properly, would he "not be accepted" by God? If, however, he was not (as God's non-acceptance of the offering had shown he was not), then "sin" was lying at his "door," waiting to pounce on him.

3. *The murder of Abel (Gen. 4:8-15)*

Cain did not profit from God's admonition, however. Quite the opposite, he now murdered Abel his brother (apparently out of jealousy) and then would not own up to it when confronted again by God (vv. 9, 10). The battle of the ages, predicted by God in Genesis 3:15, was already being waged; Satan's side (Cain) had seemingly won the first round over God's side (Abel).

But God would not let the act go unpunished. Cain would now find that the earth would not readily produce food for him (apparently in an additional sense to that of the general curse, Gen. 3:17-19). Also he would be "a fugitive and a vagabond" in the earth, having to wander without a true home.

Cain objected that this punishment was too severe, greater than he could bear, because in having merely to wander about he would have no way of protecting himself from avengers of Abel's blood. He apparently anticipated that other sons and daughters of Adam, who would be born later (Gen. 5:4), would become such avengers. As a result, God extended grace toward Cain, even in this punishment, by placing a sign on him, declaring that whoever would slay Cain would have vengeance meted out to him "sevenfold." There is no way to know what sort of sign or "mark" was used.

B. The descendants of Cain (Gen. 4:16-24)

The text now gives Cain's descendants, a lineage that must be considered in comparison with that of Seth, which will be noted in chapter 5. In Genesis 6:2, this line of Cain is called the "daughters of men" and that of Seth the "sons of God." It is said of the two lines there that intermarriage transpired, which resulted in gross sin entering into the world. In noting both lines, then, it is significant to note the propriety of these respective designations.

Before noting the lineage proper of Cain, the text states that he moved eastward to the "land of Nod," apparently soon after God's encounter with him. This land cannot be identified, and since Nod means "wandering," the thought may be that he simply lived in a region without a permanent home. There he and his wife had a child and named him Enoch. This wife could only have been a later daughter of Adam and Eve, a fact not strange in the light of the situation. Marriage to one's sister was later forbidden by God (Lev. 18:9), but here it was unavoidable. Cain also now built a city and named it after the son, Enoch. Though he was himself a wanderer, he apparently wanted a settled life for his offspring.

Verse 18 gives the names in the lineage proper from Enoch through Lamech, the latter representing the seventh generation from Adam. Nothing is known about any of these people until Lamech, but with this man came the beginning of polygamy. He had two wives, Adah and Zillah. This was wrong, for Christ makes clear that God had intended from the first a monogamous relation for a man and his wife (Matt. 19:4-6). It is true that even the righteous David, years later, had numerous wives (2 Sam. 3:2-6), but this was clearly a concession on God's part to the less-enlightened period of the Old Testament.

Verses 20-22 are significant for they indicate the beginning of three types of crafts by three sons born to Lamech (the eighth generation). The son Jabal originated the pastoral, nomadic form of life, living in tents and moving with flocks from place to place; Jubal invented instruments of music, both string ("harp") and wind ("organ" or "pipe"); and Tubal-cain introduced metallurgy, especially involving "brass and iron." The so-called copper and iron ages are known to history from a period well after this day, indicating that these early beginnings became obliterated by the later Flood.

Verses 23 and 24 give the famous "sword song" of Lamech. This song constitutes the first poetry recorded in the Bible, and it may have been one of the earliest passages written that Moses later used in his recording of the Pentateuch. The song is characterized by a spirit of defiance of God. The thought of its message is as follows: whosoever would hurt Lamech would receive, in retaliation from Lamech ten times greater vengeance than that which God had promised to avenge on any murderer of Cain. In other words, Lamech boasted to his two wives (to whom he here spoke, perhaps for want of a wider audience) that he would take care of himself ten times better than God had cared for his ancestor, Cain. This was surely arrogance in the extreme.

A summation now of the accomplishments or characteristics of Cain's line is appropriate. First, a city was built, which was a proper, earth-oriented accomplishment but nothing of a spiritual or God-centered nature; second, polygamy was started, which was definitely anti-God in spirit; third, three crafts were introduced that again were proper in themselves but were not of a spiritual or God-centered nature; and, fourth, a boastful speech was made that was even more anti-God in spirit than the polygamy. Cain's line, then, displayed nothing that had a truly God-pleasing character to it.

C. The descendants of Seth (Gen. 4:25-5:32)

The descendants of Seth are now set forth, and, in contrast to the line just presented, this line shows God-pleasing accomplishments or characteristics at frequent points.

1. *Introduction to this godly line (Gen. 4:25, 26)*

The line of Seth proper is given in chapter 5, but still in chapter 4 an introduction is presented. The purpose is to state quickly that God brought this contrasting line to existence for the purpose of replacing the one that otherwise would have developed from Abel, whom Cain slew.

Verse 25 makes this "replacement" idea clear when it states the words of Eve at the birth of Seth: God has "appointed me another seed instead of Abel." Verse 26 identifies Seth's first son, and then gives the initial God-directed note from this line, stating, "Then began men to call upon the name of the LORD." The significance seems to be that the descendants, to be listed now in chapter 5, were characterized in this way. It is significant that the name Yahweh (LORD) is used here for God. Liberal scholars have long maintained, especially in the light of Exodus 6:3,[1] that this name

[1] Exodus 6:3 speaks of Abraham, Isaac, and Jacob not knowing God by the name Yahweh but by El Shaddai. The thought is not that the name was not used by them, but that they did not appreciate or understand its true meaning in reference to God (see chap. 2, p. 28). This means that the patriarchs thought of God basically as the mighty, powerful, transcendent Being, supreme over all the earth (connotation of El Shaddai), but they did not realize adequately that He was also the gracious, condescending immanent One, who was vitally interested in their welfare (connotation of Yahweh).

was not used before the time of Moses, but it was, as this verse and others indicate.

2. *The genealogy of Seth (Gen. 5:1-32)*

a. *Further information regarding Adam (Gen. 5:1-5).* Notice should be given here that Seth's line is made important in the text by being presented as the true line from Adam. This is indicated by one of the "generation" references occurring now in verse 1 (cf. Introduction, p. 9). Appropriately, reference is made to man being made in God's image again (as it were to say that man was really descended from God), with this followed by the indication that Adam then brought forth a son, Seth, in his image (v. 3). Adam was 130 years old at the time and lived to a total of 930 years (vv. 4, 5). After the birth of Seth, Adam and Eve had other sons and daughters.

Because of the longevity of Adam and his antedeluvian descendants, the suggestion has been made that the years in reference should be understood really as months. This will not do, however, for on that basis, Seth was born when Adam was only ten years old, and, later, Methuselah was born when his father was only five (Gen. 5:21). God simply permitted man to live to a greater age during the early centuries and then gradually reduced that age following the Flood. Perhaps the development of disease played a role.

Much has been written on the subject of whether or not the genealogies of Genesis include all the generations. Most expositors believe that they do not, for the reason that it was customary for Hebrew genealogies not to include all names. Even in the genealogy of Christ, for instance, in Matthew 1:8, it is stated that "Joram [Jehoram] begat Ozias [Uzziah]," but a comparison with 2 Kings 8:24; 11:1-3; 12:1, 19-21; 14:1, 17-21 (Azariah is the same as Uzziah here), shows that between Jehoram and Uzziah actually four people lived and ruled, namely Ahaziah, Athaliah, Joash, and Amaziah. So, then, Uzziah (Azariah) was really the immediate son of Amaziah and not of Jehoram. One must realize that the Hebrew expressions, "beget" or "son of," were used in a wider sense than our present-day usage assigns to them. It is frequently stated, for instance, that Jesus was the "son of David" (see Matt. 1:1; 9:27; etc.), when actually a thousand years separated them.

b. *The genealogy proper (Gen. 5:6-32)* Ten generations are listed in this genealogy, counting Adam. The names in order of the first sons in each generation are: Adam, Seth, Enos, Cainan, Mehalaleel, Jared, Enoch, Methuselah, Lamech, Noah. Methuselah lived the longest, 969 years, and Lamech the shortest, 777 years. Of three, something special is indicated, and each is God-pleasing in kind, even as 4:26 mentions.

Of Enoch it is said that he "walked with God," for which reason "God took him," without death being experienced (v. 24, cf. Heb. 11:5). He was 365 years old at the time. This was a great honor for Enoch, even as it was for Elijah years later, when he was caught up to heaven by a "whirlwind" (2 Kings 2:11). It may be observed that Enoch was the seventh recorded generation from Adam, corresponding to the extremely boastful Lamech in Cain's line.

Of Lamech in Seth's line, it is said that he expressed hope, when Noah was born to him, that this one would bring "comfort" in respect to the toilsome work necessary as a result of the imposed curse (v. 29). The statement reveals that this man was also God-centered in his thinking, though he could have had little knowledge at the time of the way by which comfort would be brought to the world through his son (namely through deliverance for the godly line from the Flood).

Then of Noah, whose family God saved from the devastating Flood, it is stated that he was "just" and "perfect in his generations" (Gen. 6:9). Such descriptive words speak clearly for themselves.

In contrast, then, to Cain's ungodly line, every mention made of members of Seth's line is one which is God-pleasing in nature. Recognition of this fact makes understandable the designations of Genesis 6:2, "daughters of men" and "sons of God."

D. Rapid development of sin (Gen. 6:1-7)

Two views have commonly been set forth regarding the marriages of Genesis 6:1, 2: namely that they were unions between angels and earthly women, or that they were unions between the Sethite line and the Cainite line. The rationale for the latter view has been noted in the significant scriptural presentation of the two lines as "ungodly" and "godly" in character, respectively. Also, history shows that the common result of marriages between godly and ungodly people is the deterioration of the godly to be like the ungodly; and the stress of the following verses in chapter 6 is on such deterioration at this time. Besides this, verse 2 speaks of permanent marriages, not merely illicit relationship.

In favor of the "angel" view is the fact that in Job 1:6 the term "sons of God" clearly refers to angels. It seems strange, however, that God would see fit to permit angels to contribute to man's spiritual deterioration, when man was bad enough in himself not to need any outside help to make him worse. Also, Matthew 22:30 states that marriages do not occur with angels.

The marriages prompted God to speak of ceasing now to "strive" with man (v. 3). Until this point in time, God had indeed been striving with man, in an attempt to maintain a people on earth who followed Him. Adam had been made in a righteous state, but then had fallen away from God into sin. In the following generation, Cain, who lined himself on the side against God, murdered his brother Abel, who lined himself on the side for God. Then God replaced Abel with Seth, with the result that a godly line developed from Seth as an ungodly one did from Cain; but now the godly Sethite line had intermarried with the ungodly line of Cain which again brought the balance strongly on the side of ungodliness. Accordingly, God now says that the time for such striving is past and the time for judgment has come: He will give man yet 120 years and then this judgment (in the form of the flood) will come.

The Hebrew word for "giants" (v. 4) is *nephilim,* meaning literally, "fallen ones." Because this term is used for people of large size (Anakim) in Numbers 13:33, it may be that it means "large people" also here in Genesis 6:4. The last of the verse, however, suggests that this "largeness" lay in respect to reputation, as "men of renown," rather than stature. Some able people may have resulted from the Sethite-Cainite marriages and their capability could have contributed to a marked development in pride, which in turn could have helped speed the deterioration process in respect to sin.

Verses 5-7 set forth directly the extent of this deterioration, and it would be difficult to find a stronger way of describing it. God's evaluation of men saw "every imagination" of his heart as "only evil continually." Accordingly, punishment of world-wide proportions was seen necessary. Man should be destroyed, along with all forms of animal life (v. 7). This is surely a telling commentary on the extent of harm that wrong marriages can effect. It is so important that Christians marry only other Christians.

For Further Study

1. In a Bible dictionary or encyclopedia (see bibliography) read articles on: Cain, Abel, Seth, sacrifice, angels, genealogy.

2. Compare the attitudes of Cain and Abel in their offering of sacrifices.

3. How would you characterize the man Lamech, of the Cainite line?

4. Why do you believe it is that, when a believer and an unbeliever marry, the influence of the unbeliever often predominates?

5. In the light of the extent of sin as indicated in Genesis 6:5-7, do you believe that sin in the world today is worse? Explain.

Chapter 4

The Flood

(Genesis 6:8 — 9:29)

The next story in Genesis concerns God's punishment of man in the great Flood. God saw one man (Noah) and his family as still righteous in the world, gave instructions to that man regarding the coming Flood and the way he would be spared from it, and then sent the punishment which resulted in the death of all other men and all forms of animal life (except those spared along with Noah).

A. Instructions to Noah (Gen. 6:8-7:9)

1. *Preliminary matters (Gen. 6:8-13)*

In spite of the general sin and corruption in the world, Noah, of the tenth recorded generation from Adam, was still evaluated as "just" and "perfect" in his day (v. 9). The text clearly implies that it was for this reason that he now "found grace in the eyes of the LORD." All people besides his immediate family were destroyed in the Flood, meaning that he with his family alone remained on the side of God at the time.

Because Noah's family was the only one left that lived pleasing to God, it follows that God had waited in sending the Flood until this time. That is, He had not brought the Flood in punishment until man had experienced as much time as possible to repent of his sin and avoid this measure; but, at the same time, He had brought it in time to avoid having the world become devoid of all who would follow Him. It seems fair to say, in view of scriptural presentation, that God has never let the world come to a point where there have been no persons alive who have been on His side in the struggle against Satan.

By the time that God now came to Noah to give him instructions regarding the Flood and an ark he should build, Noah had seen three sons, Ham, Shem, and Japheth, born to his family. These, with their wives, besides Noah and his wife, constituted the eight persons who were saved from the Flood.

2. *Instructions regarding the ark (Gen. 6:14-7:4)*

As a way for Noah and his family to be spared from this punishment, God now told him to build an ark and gave him the design for it. It was to be similar to a large, covered barge. It should be watertight, covered both inside and out with pitch (probably bitumin from natural springs of the area), having dimensions 450 feet long, 75 feet wide, and 45 feet high (figuring eighteen inches to the cubit). It should be of three levels and it should have a window of eighteen inches in the top level for ventilation (perhaps extending all around the ark, at a width of eighteen inches).

Further, Noah should bring into the ark not only himself and his family, but also male and female representatives from all animal and bird life, along with a food supply for all. Of ordinary animals and birds, two of each kind would be sufficient, but of "clean" representatives he should bring seven. Those classified as "clean" were no doubt those suitable for sacrifice. The detailed codification of animals that were "clean" was made only in the Mosaic Law much later (Lev. 11), but animal sacrifices already had been offered by Abel (Gen. 4:4), and Noah would sacrifice them on leaving the ark (Gen. 8:20).

The last of these instructions was given after the ark had been built, and God then told Noah that he would have yet seven days for the boarding operations. After this, the rain would come for a period of forty days and nights.

Noah would have needed considerable time, of course, to build such a large boat. It may be that God's indication of 120 years as remaining for man before the Flood (Gen. 6:3) was at least in part scheduled to give Noah this time. The task would have been immense, obviously, but God's supernatural direction and instruction would have made it all possible. It should be noted also that Noah's building of the ark would have provided a forceful object lesson to back up his message for righteousness spoken of by Peter years later (2 Peter 2:5).

3. *Instructions carried out (Gen. 7:5-9)*

When Noah was 600 years old, on exactly the seventeenth day of the second month (v. 11), the ark was completed and boarding procedures were carried out. Noah and his wife, his three sons and their wives, and all the representatives of the animals and birds moved into the ark as directed. This implies, of course, a great miracle on God's part. Some of the animals and birds have had to come from great distances, and this means that these would have had to travel for some duration of time. With God, however, all things are possible; He who made all creatures can prompt activity on the part of those creatures as He wills. The number entering the ark would have been great and the sight would have been remarkable, as all the creatures mounted the gangplank to enter the giant craft.

B. The Flood (Gen. 7:10-8:14)

1. *The Flood proper (Gen. 7:10-23)*

On the appointed day, the Flood began. Water came from two basic sources: rain from above (no doubt in enormous quantity, since the time involved was forty days and nights), and from "the great deep." This last may refer to mighty convulsions in the earth's surface, with volcanic activity spewing out water and even a raising of the ocean bottoms making water spill out over the land area.

Some expositors believe that only the extent of land then known to Noah (meaning the general Mesopotamian area) was involved, holding to what is called the local-flood theory, but the story is better understood in a full universal sense. Geologic indications can be cited in support of this,[1] but more important it is required by the scriptural record. One important factor is that all men (except those in the ark) were destroyed, because all were sinners, and man almost certainly had spread out further than the comparatively small region of Mesopotamia by this time. This means that an enormous amount of water was involved in the Flood, but God could easily have raised ocean bottoms sufficiently, and possibly lowered mountain ridges an appropriate amount, so that all the earth would have been covered, even to the minimum of twenty-two and a half feet as indicated (v. 20).

2. *The duration of the Flood (Gen. 7:24-8:14)*

From the beginning of the Flood until its close (on the 27th of the second month of Noah's 601st year, 8:14), a period of one year and ten days elapsed. Numerous indications of various stages within the Flood period are given, which have been cause for considerable

---

[1] See John Whitcomb and Henry Morris, *The Genesis Flood* (Nutley, N.J.: Presbyterian and Reformed Publishing Co., 1960).

discussion by expositors. These indications seem best interpreted in the following manner:

MONTH	DAY	EVENT	NUMBER OF DAYS	REFERENCE
2	17	Entrance of ark, with water beginning to rise		7:11
3	27	Rain stops	40	7:12
7	17	Water gradually settles until ark rests on mountain	150	7:24; 8:4
10	1	Water settles more to expose mountain tops	224	8:5
11	11	Noah sends out raven and dove	264	8:6-9
11	18	Noah sends out dove again	271	8:10
11	25	Noah sends out dove for the third time	278	8:12
1	1	Noah removes the cover of the ark	314	8:13
2	27	Earth fully dry and all leave the ark	371	8:14

C. Noah leaves the ark (Gen. 8:15-22)

With the ground finally dried up fully, God told Noah to take his wife and family and all the animals and birds, and to move out from the ark. Having done so, Noah built an altar and sacrificed on it in thanksgiving to God for His supernatural protection. The sacrifice was extensive, for Noah "took of every clean beast, and of every clean fowl" in offering it. No doubt a principal reason for having included more of these clean forms of life at the first was so that this offering might be made. To have offered so many animals and birds would have taken quite some time, but the deliverance commemorated was of major importance. God was pleased with the sacrifice and promised never again to destroy all men in such a manner. He gave as a reason the fact that "the imagination of man's heart is evil from his youth." The thought is that, because man is born a sinner, he is therefore incurable in his wickedness, and punishments of this kind could not change the fact.

Interestingly, a parallel story of the Flood was discovered as a part of the Gilgamesh epic[1] from old Babylonia. It represents a deteriorated form of the original occurrence, but the similarities between the two stories are sufficient to show that they do speak of the same flood. A few sample items from the Gilgamesh story will

[1] An ancient Babylonian story.

show this similarity: a boat is made for preservation of life, though it is of larger dimensions; a man named Ut-napishtim and his family, along with representation of animal life, board the boat to escape a flood of which they are warned by supernatural beings; all human and animal life, except that on the boat, is destroyed by the flood that comes; birds (three in number, however, instead of two) are released by the man to reconnoiter at the close of the flood time; and sacrifices are offered when exit from the boat has been made.

The relation between the two accounts can be only that they are records of the same event, with the one having become corrupted into a story involving polytheism and the other remaining true under God's supernatural supervision.

D. Events immediately following the Flood (Gen. 9:1-29)

Because the Flood brought a new beginning for mankind, since only one family remained alive, it was appropriate for God to give commandments and promises to Noah in the same pattern that He had to Adam.

1. *Commandments given (Gen. 9:1-7)*

A first command was that man should fill up the earth with new progeny (v. 1; cf. 1:28). With all men destroyed, there was need for a renewal of population. This command is repeated in verse 7. A second command concerned man's relation to eating meat. He was to have dominion over the animal realm (a repetition from Adam's time, cf. 1:26) and could eat meat (something not specifically said to Adam, cf. 1:29) but only if the blood had first been taken out. Blood was symbolic of life and was, therefore, important in respect to sacrifice (cf. Heb. 9:22).

Still a third command concerned the shedding of human blood. Murder was forbidden on penalty of death for the murderer. The principal of capital punishment was laid down clearly for Noah and his posterity (vv. 5, 6). In no way did this regulation cheapen life; rather it stressed its value in God's sight.

2. *A promise given (Gen. 9:8-17)*

God followed these commands with a promise to Noah and all living beings. He would not again destroy all living beings by a flood. He had alluded to the promise already when Noah had offered the sacrifices (8:21), but now he made a point of the matter, even giving a sign that would continually remind man of it. The sign was the rainbow in the cloud (vv. 13-17). God promised that every time He saw the bow He would remember this covenant with man and not send such a universal destruction. This need not mean that no rainbow had existed before this time, for rainbows are made by the refraction of light through prisms (whether made of glass or water-drops), and even a mist can have a rainbow. The thought is probably that God now designated the bow, which had been existent, as the continuing sign of this promise.

3. *Noah's sin followed by a curse and blessings (Gen. 9:20-27)*

An episode is now recorded which resulted in some predictive statements that involved a curse and blessings.

The episode was a sad one for Noah, for he sinned in becoming intoxicated with wine and then disrobing within his tent. Ham, one of his sons, came upon his father in this naked condition, and, rather than helping his drunken father and covering him, he reported the matter to his two brothers, evidently in a disrespectful manner. The other two brothers, Shem and Japheth, reacted properly by going quickly to cover their father, taking care to show respect in not looking on him in his humiliating condition. The result was that, when Noah "awoke from his wine," he pronounced a curse and two blessings.

The curse was given as a result of Ham's sin against his father, but, surprisingly, it was not pronounced on Ham but on his son, Canaan. The reason is not clear, but it may be due to Canaan having been the most like his father of the sons, sensualistic in character. Ham had three other sons besides Canaan; they were Phut, Cush, and Mizraim (Gen. 10:6). It may be that they were not like their father, and God in this way prevented the effects of the curse coming on them through Ham, but only on Canaan.

Sometimes those who improperly believe that the black race is somehow inferior in quality argue for their view from what they call "Ham's curse." They reason that, because Ham's descendants went to Africa, the cause of Africans being black is that Ham was cursed. They should realize, however, that it was Canaan who received the curse, and he never went to Africa. It is true that Phut, Cush, and Mizraim went there, but they were not cursed. Canaan, the progenitor of the Canaanites, was the one cursed. It may be significant that the Canaanites, who did descend from him, came to be known for their sensualistic excesses, especially in religion (cf. Gen. 15:16).

A blessing was pronounced on Shem. It centered in his following the LORD (Yahweh, cf. under 4:26) as his God, for which reason

Canaan would be his "servant." The fulfillment of this predictive blessing came particularly when Abraham, of Shem's line, was selected to head God's special people Israel, and even more when Christ, in due time, was born of this same line. Implied in the fact that Canaan would be Shem's servant is the later conquest by Abraham's posterity of the Canaanite territory.

The second blessing was pronounced on Japheth, the other respectful brother. It centered in Japheth's occupying more land, though dwelling in "the tents of Shem." The thought is that Japheth would come to occupy much of the earth's area (which he did: actually all but the Middle East of the Shemites and Africa of the Hamites), but that spiritually he would be dependent on what God would do through Shem. History has proven that this did occur.

4. *Noah's death (Gen. 9:28, 29)*

Nothing more is said regarding Noah until he died, 350 years after the Flood, at the age of 950. That he lived this number of years, in comparison with Adam's 930, gives striking indication that the life span of man did not decrease at all during the whole of the antedeluvian period — Adam to Noah. There was fluctuation within the period, but no real decline.

For Further Study

1. In a Bible dictionary or encyclopedia (see bibliography) read articles on: the Flood, the ark, Noah, Ham, Shem, Japheth, sacrifice.
2. Read concerning geologic evidences for a universal flood in such books as: *The Genesis Flood,* by J. Whitcomb and H. Morris; *The World That Perished,* by J. Whitcomb; *The Flood in the Light of the Bible, Geology and Archaeology,* by A. M. Rehwinkel; *The Deluge Story in Stone,* by B. C. Nelson.
3. If God did not wish to repeat the Flood, why do you suppose He chose to send it once?
4. Try to reconstruct in your mind the magnitude of building a boat as large as the ark, especially without modern instruments and machinery.
5. Try to imagine the task of caring for all the animals and birds on the ark for the year and ten days involved.
6. What do you believe happened to all the water after the Flood? Remember that, during the Flood, the sea was just as full as the height of water on the dry land.

Chapter 5

History After the Flood

(Genesis 10:1 — 11:32)

Genesis 10 and 11 deal with history after the Flood, until the time of Abraham. Chapter 10 presents a remarkable statement of national dispersion, and chapter 11 of the significant occasion at the tower of Babel, followed by another genealogical list leading up to Abraham.

A. The table of nations (Gen. 10:1-32)

Though chapter 10 is basically an account of the descendants of Noah's three sons, Ham, Shem, and Japheth, it is more than this. It is a presentation of the origin and dispersion of national groups, for which reason it often is called a "table of nations." The rationale for the genealogy being included here is to tell how the world came to be populated again following the Flood. It presents the genealogy of Noah's three sons in the following order: Japheth, Ham, and Shem. The reason for this order is so that Shem, Israel's progenitor, might be presented last. In this way, the history given in the chapters that immediately follow — concerning the patriarchs — can be set forth without a break in thought.

The listing includes both names of ancestors of nations and of the nations themselves. Many of the nations involved, whether named as such or indicated by means of a respective ancestor, are known, while others are not. Those which are known are the more significant for notice in the discussion to follow.

1. *Descendants of Japheth (Gen. 10:1-5)*

The following groups of people are well identified from the decendants named from Japheth: "Madai" refers to the Medes; "Javan," to the Greeks (Ionians); and "Kittim," to the Cypriotes of Cyprus. Other identifications which are possible are these: "Gomer" may refer to the Cimmerians who settled in Asia Minor south of the Black Sea; "magog," to the Scythians of the lower Caucasus region; "Tubal" and "Meshach," to divisions within "Magog," especially in view of the reference to them in Ezekiel 38:2; "Tarshish," to the city of Tartessus in southern Spain, frequently mentioned in the Old Testament; and "Dodanim" (possibly the same as "Rodanim" of 1 Chron. 1:7), to the dwellers on the Aegean islands in the vicinity of Rhodes.

2. *Descendants of Ham (Gen. 10:6-20)*

The following are well identified of those named from Ham: "Cush" refers to Nubia (just north of Ethiopia); "Mizraim," to Egypt (commonly so used in the Old Testament); "Canaan," to the land of Canaan; "Sheba," to southern Arabia (cf. "Queen of Sheba," 1 Kings 10:1-13); "Babel," "Erech," and "Accad," all to cities of southern Mesopotamia; "land of Shinar," to southern Mesopotamia; "Nineveh," to the great city which later became the capital of the Assyrian Empire; "Philistim," to the Philistines; "Caphtorim," to the dwellers of Crete and possibly surrounding islands; "Sidon," to the Phoenician city of that name; "Heth," to the Hittites; "Jebusite," "Amorite," "Girgasite," and "Hivite," all to divisions of the Canaanites in Canaan; and "Arvadite" and "Hamathite," to dwellers of the Phoenician cities, Arvad and Hamath. Other possible identifications are: "Phut" to Libya, just west of Egypt; and "Calah," to Nimrud, briefly a capital of Assyria.

In this genealogy, a particular person is mentioned with stress: Nimrod, called a "mighty hunter before the LORD" (v. 9). In this context, the thought of the descriptive phrase must be that he was a "mighty hunter" of men, as he established the first kingdom which would have involved considerable physical conquest. The fact that he did this, indeed, seems to be the reason why he is featured in the story. The kingdom he set up stretched from southern Mesopotamia (Babel, Erech, Accad) north to Nineveh, which he built.

3. *Descendants of Shem (Gen. 10:21-32)*

The following are well identified of those named from Shem: "Elam" refers to the land of this name, east of Babylon; "Asshur," to Assyria; "Lud," to Lydia of Asia Minor; "Aram" to Aramaea of northern Mesopotamia; and "Eber," to the progenitor of the Hebrews through Abraham. Concerning the others, too little is known to make any reasonable identification. The reference to Peleg, that "in his days was the earth divided," is likely a reference to the division of tongues that occurred at Babel, a subject next to be considered.

B. The tower of Babel (Gen. 11:1-9)

By means of the Flood, God brought punishment on man for the sin he had committed and also appropriate discipline that man might profit for the future. Man did not profit, however, and the occasion of the tower of Babel particularly shows that he did not.

1. *The building of the tower (Gen. 11:1-4)*

The tower was constructed in the "land of Shinar," meaning lower Mesopotamia. In this region archaeologists have discovered numerous "holy" towers, called ziggurats, dating to very early time. These towers may have been copies of the original tower of Babel, though none can be identified as that first tower. The tower was made of mud brick, rather than stone, probably because no stone suitable for building exists in the area; slime (probably natural bitumin) was used for mortar.

Especially three matters show that sin had again become serious. First is the attitude of self-centeredness manifested. The people wanted to make themselves a name by building a city and this tower. The text significantly uses the first plural pronoun "us" frequently in recording the expression of their desire to this end. Then the desire indicated, of wanting the tower to "reach unto heaven," fits the same thought, for it shows their wish to insure their own eternal felicity in this way, without help from God. Their thinking in this may be linked to the existence of sacred rooms that have been found at the top of all later ziggurat towers.

Second is the reason given for the people wanting to engage in this building activity. They wanted thus to unify themselves so that they would not "be scattered abroad upon the" earth. This implies that they had in mind some directive that said they should so scatter, and God had given this in Genesis 9:1, 7, saying: "Be fruitful, and multiply, and replenish the earth." Thus they were rebelling against this clear order.

Third is the fact that God saw this occasion sufficiently serious to be cause for punishment. The Scriptures are clear that God regularly is long-suffering in bringing punishment. He had waited in bringing the Flood, until all families, with the exception of Noah's, had become wicked. He could wait no longer at that time, lest the world be left without any representative for Him living, and it may be that He waited here about as long. That He did now act in punishment, then, shows that matters had become wicked once again.

2. *The judgment of God (Gen. 11:5-9)*

God's purpose in general for now sending punishment was to bring the wickedness here demonstrated to a halt. His purpose in particular, for bringing the manner of punishment imposed, was to break up this unified, anti-God effort. When people band together, a crowd-psychology develops and actions come to be committed which few would do alone. God saw fit to bring division in the band and cause these actions to cease.

God's method of punishment was to confuse man's language. By a supernatural intervention, He made changes in the minds of the people so that they suddenly could not understand each other. One day they could, and the next they could not.

The result was that the people separated from one another and then scattered out, just as God had said they should at the first. Language is basic to any unified effort. To work together, men must understand each other. There must be communication of thought. God, of course, knew this and realized all that had to be done to break up the combine was merely to confuse the language. Probably small groups were permitted to have the same language, and they naturally would have kept together. How many different such groups there may have been, is not known. At least one such group remained yet at Babel, because from this general region (slightly south at Ur of the Chaldees), Abraham, descendant of Peleg who then lived (Gen. 1:25), was later called.

C. Genealogy of Shem to Abraham (Gen. 11:10-26)

Again a genealogy is given, this time running from Shem to Abraham. It is in part repetitious of that given in Genesis 10:22-25, where the first five names of this present list also are given: Shem, Arphaxad, Salah, Eber, and Peleg. To these, now, five others are added to get to Abraham: Reu, Serug, Nahor, Terah, and Abraham. The interest is different for this list, however, for it is given in the form used in chapter 5, where ages of the people as well as their names are indicated. This genealogy, then, is a continuation from chapter 5, not chapter 10, which as noted is more a table of nations than a genealogy.

From the genealogy of chapter 5, it was noted that Noah was the tenth generation listed from Adam, and now it appears that Abraham was the tenth after Noah. It was noted also that it was in Peleg's day that the tower of Babel incident occurred, meaning that this occasion exactly divided the ten generations after the Flood into two lists of equal length. The total list of names appears as follows:

NAME	AGE	NAME	AGE
Adam	930	Shem	600
Seth	912	Arphaxad	438
Enos	905	Salah	433
Cainan	910	Eber	473
Mahalaleel	895	Peleg	239
Jared	962		BABEL
Enoch	365 (did not die)	Reu	239
Methuselah	969	Serug	230
Lamech	777	Nahor	148
Noah	950	Terah	205
	FLOOD	Abraham	175

It may be observed that the very "artificiality" of this manner of division further suggests that omissions were made in the list (cf. discussion, chap. 3, p. 42). It could be of course that the Flood exactly divided the total generations from Adam to Abraham into two lists of ten each, and it could be that Babel divided the second list into five each, but one feels compelled to say that it is not likely. It is known that the Hebrew mind liked the idea of equal, balanced divisions in genealogical lists. This is illustrated for instance, in Matthew 1:17 where it is stated there are "fourteen generations" between Abraham and David, "fourteen" between David and the captivity, and "fourteen" from the captivity to Christ. But these equal lists of divisions can refer only to the names given, and not to the actual generations that existed, for, as was noted earlier (see chap. 3, p. 42), at least four names of kings were omitted from the middle division to make this balance of numbers.

D. The family of Terah (11:27-32)

Terah's family is now presented as further background for the story of Abraham taken up in chapter 12. Terah had three sons, Nahor, Haran, and Abraham.[1] They were not triplets, however, as

[1] Abraham's name was actually only "Abram" until changed by God, as

one might think in view of the figure "seventy years" being used for Terah's age when the three names are listed (v. 26). That figure only indicates his age when the oldest was born, who likely was Haran, since he was the first to die (v. 28). Abraham probably was the youngest, for he was seventy-five (Gen. 12:4), following the death of Terah who was 205 at his death (Gen. 11:32), meaning that Terah was 130 when Abraham was born.

Abraham married Sarai and his brother Nahor married Milcah. According to Acts 7:2-4, God's call to Abraham to leave his home town, Ur, came while Abraham yet lived in this fine city. Genesis 11:31 tells of his departure, as Terah, his father, went along and also Lot, the son of Haran and Milcah, thus a nephew to Abraham. God's directions were merely to leave Ur and go to a land He would show Abraham. The party journeyed northwest, going up the Euphrates River, and they stopped at the city of Haran in northern Mesopotamia. There Terah died. One reason the party stopped may have been because the old man had become ill in travel. The others apparently just waited until the aged patriarch could be laid to rest.

The faith of Abraham in his action of leaving Ur in this way should not be missed. He obeyed God in leaving his home city when he did not know what his destination would be. He simply trusted God to lead him to the place of His divine selection. Further, it is altogether likely that the time of this leaving occurred either during or shortly after the period when Ur was actually the leading city of the Middle East (Third Dynasty or Ur period),[2] which means that any other locality God might choose had to present less cultural advantages. Yet Abraham obeyed.

For Further Study

1. In a Bible dictionary or encyclopedia (see bibliography) read articles on: Tower of Babel, languages, Terah, Haran, Abraham.
2. Study a map showing the location of the nations set forth in the table of nations. You should find one in a book of Bible history, Bible historical geography, Bible dictionary or encyclopedia.
3. Numerous books on Biblical archaeology will show pictures of ancient ziggurats.

---

recorded in Genesis 17:5. Sarai's name also was changed at the same time (see Gen. 17:15).

[2] For evidence and discussion, see L. J. Wood, *A Survey of Israel's History*, pp. 39-42.

4. Put yourself in Abraham's place and imagine what it would have been like to be asked to leave your home like he was, and then to do it, not knowing where you were going.

Part Two:
The History of the Patriarchs

Chapter 6

Abraham (I)

(Genesis 12:1 — 16:16)

The second division of Genesis now begins. Until this point, the book has told of mankind in general, and not of a particular people, especially chosen by God, through whom to work in the world. Now it tells of such a people. Mankind generally had refused to follow God, and, therefore, God would now confine His word to one people, a people who would develop from the progeny of the man Abraham. These people would not be an end in themselves, however, but a means by which God's redeeming provision through Christ could be brought to completion, that the benefits might be taken back to all mankind again.

A. Abraham's arrival in Canaan (Gen. 12:1-20)

1. *Renewal call in Haran (Gen. 12:1-9)*

The story begins as God tells Abraham to leave Haran, now that Terah had died, and to move on to the intended destination, without indicating yet where that destination was. God added the promise at this time, however, that when he arrived at the place God would bless Abraham and bring from him "a great nation." He further promised that Abraham would be a blessing to others in this place and that God would also bless whatever people blessed him and curse those who cursed him. In other words, Abraham could rest assured that God would be near to watch out for Abraham's best interests when he came to the place of God's choosing for him.

Abraham obeyed the directive, here at Haran as at Ur, and moved on to Canaan, traveling now in a southwest direction. The distance would have been about 400 miles, added now to the approximately 1100 miles he had journeyed to reach Haran. Abraham's wife, Sarai, and nephew, Lot, continued with him, along with all their "substance" (mainly livestock) which was extensive in amount. When Abraham reached Shechem (about the geographic center of southern Canaan), God told him that he had arrived, using the promise, "Unto thy seed will I give this land." Abraham did not remain at Shechem long, however, but moved on south to the area of Bethel and Ai, and then further still, without the area being indicated.

2. *Journey to Egypt (Gen. 12:10-20)*

At this time a famine struck Canaan. God no doubt permitted it as a further test of Abraham's faith. God had promised to care for him in the land He had chosen, but this famine would have seemed to indicate the contrary. Abraham did not meet this challenge well, for he immediately left for Egypt. He apparently had learned that Egypt did not have to depend on rainfall, being watered by the Nile River.

One sin often leads to another. It did here with Abraham; since he failed to trust God in Canaan, he now sinned still more grievously in telling an outright lie regarding his wife. He and his wife agreed to state that she was his sister, rather than his wife. The reason was that Abraham feared the Egyptians might kill him for his wife, since she was attractive. There was some truth to the story, since Sarai was Abraham's half sister (Gen. 20:12), and also it should be realized that the two had earlier agreed on this procedure when and if such a situation would occur (Gen. 20:12).

In spite of these offsetting facts, however, one cannot admire Abraham at this time. Surely this was not a period of strong faith in his life. He had done well in traveling all the way to Canaan, but somehow, having arrived, he lost out on the high point he had manifested earlier. In this lie, he actually was showing that he was willing to have his wife taken by another man, rather than risk death on his own part. This was not exactly an exhibition of gallantry. If he had so feared what might happen to him in Egypt, this should only have been the more reason to trust God and stay in Canaan, where God had assigned him.

As Abraham had feared, the Egyptians did find Sarai attractive. In this he had been right. She was taken to the court of the Egyptian Pharaoh and apparently added as one more in his harem. God intervened now, however. He struck Pharaoh's house with "great plagues," and somehow conveyed information to the ruler regarding Sarai's true relation to Abraham. Then Pharaoh, quite properly incensed at what had transpired, bid Abraham leave his country and take his wife with him. He further provided an escort, probably to make sure that Abraham left.

B. Return to Canaan (Gen. 13:1-18)

1. *Return to Bethel (Gen. 13:1-4)*

When Abraham returned to Canaan, he went directly to the area of Bethel and Ai where he had built an altar on first entering the land. Verse 4 states that "there Abram called on the name of the LORD." The significance is that here Abraham restored his fellowship with God. He had been taught his lesson in Egypt, had come to realize the folly of his actions, and now desired the former life of faith-dependence to be renewed.

2. *Prosperity a problem (Gen. 13:5-13)*

Both Abraham and Lot were rich in livestock. Wealth of the day was measured largely in the number of animals one owned. These two men had so many, along with the host of servants to tend them, that they now found it difficult to live together. Pasture evidently was insufficient and tending personnel began to quarrel over what there was. Therefore, Abraham suggested that the two separate, and he gave Lot his choice of which part of the land he wanted. Actually, this was Abraham's prerogative, for he was the senior member of the company, and Lot should have recognized this and responded accordingly. But Lot was not the magnanimous person his uncle was and he was quite ready to exercise the privilege granted. Abraham is to be admired for giving the privilege, while Lot is to be discredited for accepting it.

Then Lot erred further in the choice he made. He saw the "well-watered" plain of the Jordan and chose to go there. This lowland area looked good to him, in contrast to the hill country of Bethel and Ai where they then were. People lived in the valley, for there crops grew well and grazing was good. Lot would have no problem finding pasture. And, anyhow, Lot liked to live where people were, as the following story clearly indicates. Here he would find them, which he had not been able to do in the sparsely populated highlands. But finding people would also mean finding their sin, and this would be his undoing, as the story goes on to indicate.

In this connection, it should be observed that, though today the Jordan area near the Dead Sea is arid and unattractive, archaeologists have found that it was just as the story here presents it at this early time. The remains of many cities have been found, all of which came to an end in the nineteenth century B.C. At that time the character of the land changed completely, quite possibly in connection with the destruction meted out on Sodom and Gomorrah and "all the plain" (Gen. 9:24, 25).

3. *Promise to Abraham (Gen. 13:14-18)*

Though Lot wanted the lowlands, Abraham was quite content to remain in the hill country. He no doubt would have chosen it, even if Lot would not have accepted the right of first choice. The hill country, being sparse in population, gave Abraham room to move without infringing on the rights of others, and he needed much land for his large flocks and herds. He had certainly been hurt, however, by the disrespect shown him by Lot, and God apparently now saw him in need of encouragement. God appeared to him to repeat the promise that this land, where he was then living, would indeed become the home of his posterity. This posterity, He added, would become in size like the "dust of the earth." With the promise given again, Abraham now moved south to the "plain of Mamre" near Hebron, where he was to spend many years. He built an altar to the Lord here also, as an evidence of the faith he felt in his heart.

C. Kings from the east (Gen. 14:1-24)

An episode of quite a different nature is found inserted in the sacred text at this point. It concerns the entrance into the region of Canaan by four kings from the east (lower Mesopotamia) and their battles with Canaanite cities in the area south of the Dead Sea. The reason for this insertion is that Lot came to be involved with them, when he was captured in their defeat of Sodom.

1. *Lot captured in the defeat of Sodom (Gen. 14:1-13)*

The four eastern kings were named Amraphel, Arioch, Chedorlaomer, and Tidal. They were a long ways from home, having traveled all the way from the general area where Abraham had lived. At one time liberal scholars scoffed at the story, claiming that kings this early in time just did not go this far to do battle. Today, however, archeologists have shown that, even before this time, kings like Sargon and Narim-sin from this same area, made campaigns at comparable distances. It is significant further that, though these particular kings cannot be identified with any known persons of secular history, their names have been found as used by others of the general time, indicating that the story does fit nicely into the environmental setting of the day.

These four made war with five kings who all seem to have ruled in the vicinity of the southern end of the Dead Sea, among whom were the kings of Sodom and Gomorrah. These five kings had been subject to Chedorlaomer for the prior twelve years, but they had now revolted, and he had come, with the three helpers named, to put down their revolt. He campaigned at various points in the general area at first and then engaged the five kings in a pitched battle "in the valley of siddim" where there were "slimepits." These slimepits likely were natural bitumin wells of the region, which evidently played some part in the outcome of the struggle. The outcome was that the five kings were defeated by the easterners, their cities devastated, and many of the people, including Lot, taken captive. News of this great loss reached Abraham through one who escaped.

2. *Rescue of Lot by Abraham (Gen. 14:14-17)*

Abraham's reaction was to go immediately to Lot's rescue. Lot had earlier wronged him, but Abraham did not let this hinder him in the decision of the hour. He made the decision, too, even though he could not begin to assemble an army that would compare with that of the enemy. He had only 318 of his own servants, along with three of his neighbors, Mamre, Eshcol, and Aner. That he had as many as 318 servants is significant as to his personal wealth, and that these three neighbors were willing to go with him shows that he had good community relations. But this was certainly a pitifully small number to go against an enemy that had just defeated five kings. Abraham truly manifested courage in this act, along with his willingness to overlook the wrong of Lot. Even more, he gave evidence of a great faith in God, for it could be only by divine intervention that he could possibly be successful. Not only were his men few in number, but they were fully untrained, and what they may have used for weapons one can only guess. Abraham went, however, depending on God to accomplish through these few the great task before him.

Notice should be made, further, that it is in this text where the term "Hebrew" is first used in the Bible. It probably comes from the name of an ancestor, "Eber." Because "Hebrew" is close etymologically to the term "Habiru," which has been found used in many texts for a certain class of people of the Middle East during the second millennium B.C., some scholars have sought a relationship between them. Too many problems have arisen, however, to make the relationship likely.

Abraham's small army caught up with the easterners at "Dan." This is hardly the Dan of later time, which was given this name at the time of its conquest by the tribe of Dan (Judg. 18:1-29), and which also would have been out of the way for these four kings as they made their way home. It more likely was another city of the name, such as Dan-jaan (2 Sam. 24:6), which appears to have been in Gilead and on the way these kings could be expected to have taken.

At this Dan, Abraham met and defeated the larger enemy force. He was able to free Lot and the other captives, and to recover the captured "goods." What tactic Abraham may have used to do this is not indicated, but of course the major reason was the blessing of God.

3. *Meeting Melchizedek and the king of Sodom (Gen. 14:18-24)*

On returning from this fine victory, Abraham was met by two kings. One was Melchizedek, "king of Salem" (Jerusalem). "Salem" means "peace"; "Melchizedek" means "king of righteousness." This king was also a priest, thus combining the religious and secular under one head. More important, as priest, he served the true God, "the most high God," and Abraham recognized this. How this king had come to this faith is not indicated, but somehow he had, possibly through an earlier contact by Abraham.

Melchizedek recognized the courageous deed of Abraham and met him with "bread and wine"; he also pronounced a blessing on him in his capacity as priest. In the blessing he expressed the thought that God had truly been the One who had "delivered" the enemy into Abraham's hand. As a result, Abraham in turn gave Melchizedek "tithes of all" that he had seized from the enemy. Apparently he saw this priest as a representative of God and, therefore, by this act gave back to God the recognized tithe of what God had just given to him. This makes the fact rather clear that God had established the principal of the tithe prior to this time, thus well before the giving of the law through Moses. Because of this interaction between Abraham and Melchizedek, the latter is made a prefigurement of Christ both in Psalm 110:4 and Hebrews 7:1-22.

The other King was "the king of Sodom," who apparently had not personally been either killed or captured in the earlier battle.

This king also came to meet Abraham, and, out of gratitude, now urged Abraham to keep all the material "goods" that had been recovered and to give him only the people. Abraham replied, however, that he had promised God he would not accept "a thread even to a shoelatchet" from the king, lest people would say that this king had "made Abram rich." The only exception would be that which his servants had already eaten of the foodstuffs and a portion that rightfully belonged to his three neighbors, Mamre, Eshcol, and Aner, who had helped. Besides this, of course, Abraham could not have returned the tenth of the "goods" that he had just given to Melchizedek.

Abraham's reason for rejecting this material wealth (which probably was of considerable amount) was no doubt to make clear his dependency on God alone. People could see that he was rich anyhow, without this additional gift from the Sodomite king, and Abraham wanted them to recognize that it was solely because of God's gracious benefits. This would be a testimony to them that the true God was the God in whom they also ought to trust. Abraham is to be highly commended, for though he already had plenty, one is always tempted to want more. In fact, the normal rule is that the more a person has the more he wants. Abraham, however, was able to rise above this natural desire and to refuse the gift.

D. Covenant restated through a vision (Gen. 15:1-21)

God now saw fit to reassure Abraham through a vision concerning His promise regarding a nation-size posterity and the possession of Canaan as the land of inheritance.

1. *Abraham's concern (Gen. 15:1-3)*

The need for this reassurance was prompted by some anxiety on Abraham's part. God appeared to him in a vision, and in this vision Abraham expressed the concern that his heir would have to be his servant, "Eliezer of Damascus," since he had no child of his own. Discoveries at Nuzi of tablets dating only shortly after this time of Abraham show that Abraham was referring to a common custom of the day. A childless couple would adopt a servant and then he would be their heir, unless a natural child should later be born to them, who would then take the precedence.

2. *God's initial response (Gen. 15:4-7)*

God immediately responded to Abraham (still in vision, as is the entire chapter), that Eliezer would not be his heir, but that Abraham would have his own son. God reinforced this assertion by first having Abraham look at the stars above and then giving the promise that his posterity actually would grow to a number comparable in size. He added that it had been for this reason that Abraham had been brought out from "Ur of the Chaldees" in the first place.

3. *God's confirming sign (Gen. 15:8-17)*

Abraham now asked God for a confirmation of the truth of these wonderful promises, and God in grace gave him one. He told Abraham to bring before him "an heifer," "a she goat," "a ram," "a turtledove," and a "young pigeon." Abraham did so. Then Abraham — no doubt following further instruction given — divided each of the three animals into two halves, apparently laying all end to end in a line, while leaving the two birds whole (v. 10). This corresponded to a rite recognized in the Middle East at the time. Animals would thus be cut in half, at the time of making a covenant between two parties, and the parties would then walk between the halves to symbolize themselves as united by the bond of common blood. In the instance mentioned here, as Abraham finished laying the divided animals in place, birds of the air suddenly descended on them and Abraham had to drive them away. That this is recorded suggests that these birds symbolized obstacles that would arise for Abraham in the carrying out of God's promises.

With this done, God began to speak at some length to Abraham, as Abraham, still in vision, saw the sun go down and sensed a "deep sleep" come upon him. The thought of what God said was that Abraham's posterity would truly suffer obstacles, as they would be compelled to serve in a strange land "four hundred years," but that they would in time come back into this promised land, "when the iniquity of the Amorites [Canaanite inhabitants]" was full.

When the promise had been given, the sign involving the slain animals was given. God caused a "smoking furnace, and a burning lamp" to pass between the divided animals. This "furnace" (stove of the day) with the flame burning up from it represented God in His divine justice. That He alone passed between the halves of the animals, rather than He with Abraham, symbolized that God was assuming sole responsibility in the covenant just presented. It also carried the representation that, though Israel would suffer for as long as 400 years, God would be near, in the midst of His people, during this time. It was the type of sign that would have been highly meaningful to Abraham in this time of anxiety.

4. *The extent of the promise (Gen. 15:18-21)*

The closing verses of the chapter enlarge on the extent of territory God had in mind for Abraham's posterity to inherit. It would stretch from "the river of Egypt" to "the river Euphrates," and include all the peoples listed in verses 19-21, who were either divisions of Canaanites or peoples who settled among the Canaanites. The "river of Egypt" in view may be either the *nahal Mitzraim* (brook of Egypt), which flows into the Mediterranean at present El Arish, or possibly the Nile River. It is difficult to say which is the more likely, but whichever was intended, the main purpose was to say that the intended area would reach from Egypt to the Euphrates. Fulfillment of this promise was approximated in the day of David, but a complete fulfillment will be realized only in the millennial day to come, when Christ will be King of His people.

E. The birth of Ishmael (Gen. 16:1-16)

1. *A wrong suggestion (Gen. 16:1-3)*

When ten years had passed in Canaan (v. 3), since the promise of a large posterity had first been given, Abraham and Sarai became impatient for the first evidence of such a progeny. Their impatience can be understood by any parent today, but it was wrong in the sight of God. If God had promised a posterity, it would come, whether ten years had passed or not. Sarai made a suggestion to Abraham on how he might have a son and her plan was wrong. She suggested that Abraham "go in unto" her handmaid, Hagar, and have a son by her. Though this procedure was wrong, still the fact that Sarai made it must be judged in the light of an accepted custom of the day. The Nuzi tablets show that it was a wife's obligation to give children to her husband, and that if she could not bear them herself she should do so through her handmaid.

2. *Resulting trouble (Gen. 16:4-6)*

Abraham followed his wife's suggestion, and Hagar conceived. When she did, however, she became disrespectful of Sarai (evidently because she had been able to conceive when Sarai had not), and Sarai now complained to Abraham. Abraham gave her permission to do with Hagar as she wished, and, when Sarai treated her harshly, Hagar fled and started for Egypt, her home country.

3. *Hagar is met by the Angel of the Lord (Gen. 16:7-12)*

When Hagar had gotten as far as Shur (an area south of Palestine, on the way to Egypt), she was met by the "angel of the LORD," and He bid her to return to Sarai and submit to her authority. He also promised that her posterity would become very large, and told her to name the son to be born, Ishmael (meaning, "God hears"). He said that the child would become a "wild man" and that he would find frequent opposition from those among whom he would live. The term "wild man" (literally, "wild ass of a man") was probably not intended as an insult to the son, but rather an indication that he would be free and roving in spirit, like the wild ass. That he would find frequent opposition is no doubt still finding an aspect of fulfillment today in the continuing struggle between Arabs and Jews. The Arabs are descendants of many others besides Ishmael, but he would have been one of their ancestors.

This occasion presents the first appearance of the "angel of the LORD" in Scripture. From this text and others where He appears later (see e.g. Gen. 18:1-33), it is clear that this One was a manifestation of God Himself (specifically the Second Person of the Godhead), who in appropriate instances assumed a temporary natural body.[1] For this divine Being to appear to a person here on earth, then, was a distinct honor for that person. That God should have given this honor to Hagar may seem surprising, but it indicates that He had a tender concern for her.

4. *Response of Hagar (Gen. 16:13-16)*

Hagar's response shows her to have been a person of faith, no doubt having come to place faith in the true God as a result of being in Abraham's home. She identified her Visitor with God and called His name, "Thou God seest me," indicating her recognition that God had seen her and had been gracious to her. As a result, a nearby well, where she had stopped at the time, was called "Beer-lahai-roi," meaning, "The well of the Living One who sees me."

Hagar now returned to her mistress, and in due course she bore a son and named him Ishmael as instructed. Abraham was eighty-six years old at the time. No doubt Hagar told Abraham of her meeting with the Angel, and this would have helped to teach him how improper had been the action of both himself and his wife toward Hagar. She should not have been used as a way of "helping out" God in respect to the promise of a progeny, and she should not have been driven from home when a son had been conceived.

[1] For further discussion, see chapter 7, p. 76.

Abraham should have waited for God's own time to give him a son and simply trusted rather than become anxious.

For Further Study

1. In a Bible dictionary or encyclopedia (see bibliography) read articles on: Shechem, Bethel, Ai, Sarah, Sodom, Dead Sea, Melchizedek, Hagar, Ishmael.
2. Do you believe Abraham was right in taking Terah with him from Ur and then stopping at Haran and waiting until his aged father died?
3. By putting yourself in Abraham's place, when famine struck just after reaching Canaan, try to reconstruct the thinking that went through his mind.
4. Do the same for the time when Abraham learned that Lot had been captured by the four eastern kings, followed by his decision to try to free Lot.
5. What does Abraham's refusal of the Sodomite king's offer say as to the character of Abraham?
6. Why do you believe God stated His promises to Abraham so many times?
7. What lessons can be learned from the experience of Abraham and Sarai with Hagar?

Chapter 7

Abraham (II)

(Genesis 17:1 — 20:18)

Thirteen more years were to pass before God would again appear to Abraham. During this time Hagar remained in the home and Ishmael grew to his early teen years. The time must have seemed long, when Abraham and Sarai desired a son so much. But finally God did come to them again, this time to promise specifically the birth of their own son Isaac.

A. Further reassurance of the promises (Gen. 17:1-27)

1. *The promises restated (Gen. 17:1-8)*

God began this occasion of revelation by first identifying Himself as "the Almighty God *(El Shaddai).*" Though the exact etymology of *Shaddai* is disputed, its contextual employment makes the meaning "almighty" all but certain. God wanted Abraham to realize that God was all powerful and fully able to bring about the fulfillment of all promises He would make. The additional word of admonition by God, "Walk before me, and be thou perfect," was to tell Abraham that this manner of conduct would be conducive to the promises being kept in the fullest possible sense.

God then gave the great promises once again, declaring that Abraham's posterity would become large, so that he would actually become a "father of many nations," with even kings being included, and that the land where Abraham lived would truly be "an everlasting possession for this posterity." This time an additional stress was made on the fact that the covenant would be "everlasting" in duration. Besides this, God made a change in Abraham's own name; whereas he had been "Abram" (meaning, "high father") until this time, he would now be "Abraham" (meaning, "father of a multitude"). The name change was in keeping with the promises.

2. *An obligation assigned (Gen. 17:9-14)*

God now set forth an obligation on Abraham's part, which was to apply both to himself and his posterity. It was that every male member of Abraham's household was to be circumcised. It was to be performed on male children at the age of eight days, and was to apply whether the one involved was of Abraham's own family or whether "bought with money" (slave-servants). This rite was to be a "token" (evidence) that the one circumcised belonged to Abraham's household, the lineage of which in time would form the special nation here promised. In other words, by this sign, Abraham's posterity would be marked off from other people, so that distinctness could be maintained. The rite was so important in God's sight that those who would neglect it should be "cut off" as a posterity member.

It should be realized that circumcision was not new in the world of that time. Other peoples have been identified who also practiced the rite, but here God adopted it as a particular sign of designation for His people.

3. *The particular promise of a son (Gen. 17:15-22)*

God at last became very specific in His promise. The first of this promised posterity would now be born to Abraham. Before stating the matter proper, however, God made a change also in Sarai's name. Whereas she had been called "Sarai" (meaning uncertain) she would now be called "Sarah," which means "princess." The thought was that as a "princess" she would become a mother of nations. The time was right for the name change because the moment for the birth of the first in the line was at hand.

The fact of this birth God now proceeded to declare. Sarah would truly bear a son and through him she would become a "mother of nations." Abraham responded improperly at this announcement. He actually laughed at the words, though at the same time he fell on the ground apparently in adoration. It must be that his feelings were mixed, not being able to see how he, at the age of one hundred and his wife at ninety, could possibly have a child. In this confused state, he voiced a surprising request, "O that Ishmael might live before thee!" This announcement of another son seems to have made him think of the future of Ishmael, whom he apparently had grown to love. He desired that God know that Abraham wished only the best also for this son.

God's response to Abraham was twofold. First, He asserted again that Sarah should indeed have a son (in spite of what Abraham considered an impossibility) and even indicated his name, "Isaac," meaning, "one laughs." Second, He spoke of Ishmael, thus giving deference to Abraham's concern, saying that he too would be fruitful in progeny, which would result also in a "great nation" (the Ishmaelites) being formed. The covenant of promise would be made with Isaac, however, whom Sarah would bear one year later.

4. *Obedience rendered (Gen. 17:23-27)*

When God completed His instructions, Abraham obeyed them in having all the male members of his house circumcised, including himself and Ishmael. Abraham was ninety-nine at the time, and Ishmael was thirteen. Since the directive included all slave servants, there were many more slave servants circumcised than family members (really only the two).

B. Abraham and the Angel of the Lord (Gen. 18:1-33)

Once more a clear revelation concerning the coming birth of Isaac was made and this time it was made directly to Abraham through a second appearance of the Angel of the Lord.

1. *The visit of "three men" (Gen. 18:1-16)*

The Angel of the Lord was accompanied in this visit by two others, who evidently were ordinary angels, all three being called simply at first "three men" (v. 2). It is clear that the One was truly the Angel of the Lord (theophany) for He is called "LORD" *(Yahweh)* in verses 1, 13, 14, etc., and also He referred to Himself as "I" when speaking in the capacity of God (vv. 17, 26, etc.). The three heavenly visitors approached Abraham as he sat near his tent at Mamre, and he properly offered them rest and refreshment, which they accepted. The food Abraham prepared was liberal in amount; it included a large quantity of bread and an entire calf for meat, besides butter and milk.

Either during or after the meal, one of the visitors (no doubt, the Angel of the Lord), gave the promise that in due time Sarah truly would have a son, repeating the thought of the prior chapter, apparently for the sake of emphasis. Sarah, though inside the tent, was able to hear the words and she "laughed within herself," believing the words could not be true. Interestingly, it had been Abraham who had laughed in chapter 17. The Angel knew she laughed and brought a rebuke, saying, "Is anything too hard for the LORD?"

Sarah now voiced a denial that she had laughed, but this only made her conduct the more reprehensible.

The reason for the laughter of both Abraham and Sarah was that Sarah was past the age of having children. No doubt the two reasoned that, if God wanted them to have a child, He would have made this possible while Sarah yet had ability to bear children. It is quite clear, however, that God had purposely waited so that, when Isaac should be born, the importance of the birth and the fact that God had been supernaturally responsible for it (being by miracle) would be the more impressed on the parents' minds.

2. *The revelation concerning Sodom (Gen. 18:17-22)*

At this point, the three heavenly visitors and Abraham started to walk in the direction of Sodom. As they walked, the Angel of the Lord informed Abraham of the impending destruction of Sodom. The rather unusual manner by which the text tells of the Angel doing this intends to convey the following thought: God was interested in Abraham, as the father of the nation who would inherit all this land, and He wanted to express His desire that Abraham know why the coming punishment on Sodom was necessary, so that he would not be confused in thinking that possibly the same might happen to all the land so promised. Abraham should understand, then, that this punishment was only because of the "cry" of Sodom (cry for punishment due to sin); thus it was a punishment for that part of the land only and not all of it. Though the actual term "destruction" was not used by the Angel, the thought was made clear enough so that Abraham now began an unusual plea for Sodom's deliverance.

3. *Abraham intercedes for Sodom (Gen. 18:23-33)*

This plea was given after the two ordinary angels had continued in their walk to Sodom, with Abraham and the Angel of the Lord having stopped. Abraham stepped nearer the Angel, in a gesture evidently of deep sincerity, to intercede in Sodom's behalf. Certainly he had a primary interest in Lot in so doing (which further shows his magnanimous character toward this undeserving nephew), but no doubt also an interest in the preservation of people generally in the city. His intercession was based on the thought that a certain number of righteous people in a city should be reason to spare that city. Abraham apparently had noticed the closing words of the Angel's declaration, which, in effect, said that He was going to "go down now" and determine whether the "cry" for punishment had been serious enough to call for the punishment (v. 21).

Abraham started with the number "fifty," asking if this would be a small enough number of righteous people to make the punishment unnecessary. The Angel replied that it would be. Then Abraham reduced the number to forty-five and then forty and finally to as few as ten. The reply each time was that even as few as any of these numbers would be people enough. Abraham did not go lower than ten, no doubt believing that surely a city where Lot lived would have at least this many whom God could consider righteous. Since the city was destroyed, it is clear that this many were not found, which means that really Abraham's intercession yielded no tangible result.

The implication of the text, however, is that God was pleased with Abraham's attempt. He made the intercession in full humility and demonstrated true compassion for others, which always is commendable. The fact that as few as ten righteous people did not live in Sodom, however, provides a sad commentary on the ineffectiveness of Lot's witness.

C. The destruction of Sodom (Gen. 19:1-38)

1. *Lot is rescued by the angels (Gen. 19:1-23)*

The story now concerns the visit of the two ordinary angels to Lot's home in Sodom. Evening had fallen when they arrived, and they found Lot sitting "in the gate of Sodom." Because city gates of the day served as places of community meeting (cf. Prov. 31:23; Ruth 4:1), the fact that Lot was there suggests that he was involved in Sodom's activities, as an accepted, well-known citizen. From this and the fact that his witness had been so poor in the city, the conclusion follows that he had not learned any lesson from his previous capture by the four kings. It had been easy to take up with the ways of Sodom once again and just be one of the crowd. He is a picture of a Christian (cf. 2 Peter 2:7: "just Lot") who lives close to the world and does not want to be separated or distinguished from it.

Lot was courteous to his two visitors and properly invited them to his house to spend the night, even urging them to do so when they at first appeared to decline. During the evening, wicked men of the city came to the house and wanted to "know" his visitors. To protect the two, Lot offered the men his own two daughters. Lot can be commended for wanting to protect the visitors, but not for offering his daughters. One has to wonder whether Sodom had any police force or a sense of decency at all, that Lot thought his only alternative was to make such an offer. The fact that he did this says much regarding the morals of Sodom and it says much as to his own standards, as well as that of his daughters. The thoughts which later led to their incest with their father (Gen. 19:22-38) evidently had been planted long before.

Even this radical offer, however, did not satisfy the ruffian group who wanted the two visitors. As a result, Lot suddenly found himself being rescued from the wild crowd by the two visitors themselves, as they moved quickly to draw him back into the house and smite the wicked mob with blindness. It may be that it was at this time when Lot first recognized his visitors to be more than ordinary mortals like himself. He must have been doubly ashamed at the realization of their heavenly origin.

With this experience fresh in mind, Lot was now urged by the two angels to leave Sodom quickly, warning him that the city was about to be destroyed. They instructed him also to bring his family with him. No doubt Lot had mixed emotions regarding these words at first. He had become much involved with Sodom and liked to live there, in spite of its wickedness. His own inner sense of right, however, especially in the light of the heavenly origin of those who warned him, prevailed and he chose to leave.

When he tried to persuade his family to do the same, however, he was less than successful. He was able to make his wife and two daughters willing, but not his sons-in-law. They clearly were sinful men of the city, quite in sympathy with all that was being done, and they now made light of Lot's warning and would not leave. The following morning, even Lot himself tended to linger too long in the city with which he had become enamored, and the angels had to lay "hold" on him and the three women to compel them to leave quickly, God thus "being merciful unto him" (v. 16).

Having brought the four outside the city, the angels instructed them to flee to the "mountain," but Lot objected to this. He wanted to go instead to a nearby city, since it was "a little one" (v. 20). Clearly, Lot enjoyed city life, rather than the loneliness of a mountain. If he had to leave the large city of Sodom, he still wanted to go to a small one. He had experienced trouble with this desire from the first. He had wanted the Jordan valley, where there were people, but these people had been the ones who had brought him his sad spiritual condition. He still had not learned his lesson.

The angels gave him permission to make this change in their directions, though no doubt reluctantly, knowing that it would not work to his good. At this point the angels may have disappeared, for they are not heard from again. Lot and his family then went to the city, named Bela (Gen. 14:2, 8), which now came to be called Zoar. Its identity remains unknown. Even the location of Sodom and Gomorrah is not known for sure, but the best guess still is that it was what is now beneath the water of the present southern end of the Dead Sea.[1]

2. *The destruction of Sodom (Gen. 19:24-29)*

As Lot entered small Zoar, God obliterated Sodom and Gomorrah, along with other cities "and all the plain" by a rain of "brimstone and fire" (v. 24). Since God normally uses natural means when available to do His work, it may be that this "brimstone and fire" was composed of natural gasses and inflamable substances of the area, possibly released in great quantity by an appropriately timed earthquake, and then ignited. Whatever the means, the destruction was total, and the area both north and south of the Dead Sea shows evidence of a marked change dating from this general time. Prior to the time it was heavily populated, but following that day it became, and still is, a forsaken waste region. A miracle was performed, of course, whether by the timely use of natural means or by supernaturally produced destructive elements.

A sad aspect in the destruction was that Lot's wife, though she had properly fled with her husband, now became a casualty. As the four moved away from the burning city, she "looked back" and was killed. The Hebrew includes the element that she looked back "from behind him," suggesting that she had separated herself from Lot at the time, perhaps having turned back to see better the destruction of the city she loved. She had probably been born there, in distinction from Lot, and may have had a deeper love for the place than he.

The result was that she "became a pillar of salt," meaning probably that she was near enough to the destructive rain that she was overcome herself by it and became encrusted with the salty residue. So encased, her body could have remained existent for some time, thus providing a continuing object lesson of the seriousness of not

---

[1] Recently, however, interesting discoveries of five city-sites have been made just to the east and south of the Dead Sea, two of which could be Sodom and Gomorrah. See *Bible and Spade,* 3 (Summer, 1974), 65-89 for discussion.

obeying God fully. The directive of the angels had been, "Look not behind thee" (v. 17), and Lot's wife had disobeyed.

Verses 27-29 add the note that Abraham, as he rose early the same morning, could see the smoke of Sodom's destruction in the eastern distance. It would have made him realize, to his great regret certainly, that there had not been ten righteous people in the city after all. It is stated, however, that Lot's deliverance was because God "remembered Abraham," which means that Abraham's intercession of the prior day had not been totally in vain. Though God did not spare Sodom, He did spare Abraham's nephew and family, in whom Abraham's interest lay mainly. Carnal Lot was indebted to his spiritual uncle that day without knowing it.

3. *Lot and his two daughters (Gen. 19:30-38)*

The capstone to Lot's carnal conduct came when his two daughters contrived to have incestual relations with him in a cave on a mountain. Lot did move out of Zoar and to the mountain after all, as the angels had directed. He may have feared that Zoar might be destroyed too. He now made his home in the "cave," certainly a humbling experience after what probably had been a fine home in Sodom. He had lost all his wealth in the destruction of Sodom, and a cave was apparently all he could afford. Sin indeed takes its toll.

There, in this cave, his two daughters, childless and widowed, planned to have illicit relations with him so that they might each have a child. The older of the two suggested the plan and carried through with it first. They made their father drink wine until he was intoxicated — no doubt acting on knowledge concerning their father they had learned back in Sodom — and then the older came to him one night and the younger on the next night, both having relations with him. Each conceived a child as was desired, and the older gave birth to a son she named Moab and the younger to one she named Ben-ammi. From these came the later Moabites and Ammonites, who continued for years as enemies of Israel. What remorse Lot must have felt when he realized what his daughters had done to him, and how this really only represented the depth of humiliation to which he had come. He now had so little from life, in comparison with his wealthy uncle who had given him first choice many years before. He had indeed chosen wrongly when he had selected the sinful ways of the Jordan valley.

D. Abraham's sin at Gerar (Gen. 20:1-18)

The story now reverts to Abraham and once more shows him in a bad light. One feature of the Bible is that it sets forth the sins of people as well as their righteous deeds. Abraham here again sinned in respect to his wife as he had in Egypt years before.

1. *God warns Abimelech (Gen. 20:1, 2)*

For some reason Abraham now moved from Mamre (Hebron) and went westward to the city of Gerar, in southwestern Canaan. He told people of the area that Sarah was his sister, as he had the Egyptians nearly twenty-five years earlier, with the result that Abimelech, the king of the city, took her into his palace as had Egypt's Pharaoh.

2. *God warns Abimelech (Gen. 20:3-7)*

God intervened once more for Sarah and warned Abimelech in a dream that Sarah was Abraham's wife and that he was wrong in thinking of her as belonging to him. In the dream, Abimelech properly protested his innocence and God recognized it, but instructed him not to "touch" Sarah. Instead, he was to restore her to her husband.

Notice should be made that Abraham is here called a "prophet" by God, the first instance in Scripture of the use of the word. The word "prophet" *(nabi')* means one who "speaks for God" (cf. Exod. 7:1 with Exod. 4:14-16). Abraham received communications from God and spoke for Him (like Moses, Deut. 18:15).

3. *Abimelech confronts Abraham (Gen. 20:8-13)*

Abimelech took proper steps the following morning to carry out God's directive. He first assembled his servants and warned them concerning Sarah and then confronted Abraham, asking why he had made this misrepresentation. Abraham told him the truth, that he had feared possible harm to himself if the people knew he was Sarah's husband. He then added the note, not made in the earlier instance, that he and Sarah had agreed to this procedure should they come into a situation that they felt called for it. He further stated that his falsehood had really contained an element of truth, for Sarah was at least his half-sister.

This degree of truth, however, in no way made Abraham's action right. The principal wrong lay in not claiming Sarah as his wife, because it could cause her to be violated by other men. Abraham's action in this, in view of his excellent character in other respects, is difficult to understand. One would be tempted to say he was cowardly, but surely he had been anything but cowardly in his action of pursuing the four-king army from the east. One can only say that Abraham, like so many of God's children, had a weakness, and it continued to appear in his life.

4. *Abimelech's generosity toward Abraham (Gen. 20:14-18)*

Abimelech graciously requited Abraham's wrong by giving him rich gifts. This is the case of a pagan outdoing a child of God in a virtue which is pleasing to God. He gave Abraham sheep, oxen, male and female servants, besides restoring his wife. He also gave him permission to live in his land wherever he wished. Abimelech told Sarah why he responded in this way to Abraham: the gift was for "a covering of the eyes." By this he probably meant that he thus wanted to appease Abraham for the wrong done in taking Sarah into his palace (though indeed he had been innocent in so doing, as he had said earlier). Abraham's eyes would thus be "covered" in respect to the wrong. Abimelech's reaction was quite in contrast to that of the Egyptian Pharaoh earlier, who had summarily dismissed Abraham from his country.

Abraham's response, now, was to pray for Abimelech, and God then healed the man's household, the members of which had been made sterile because of Sarah. No doubt it had been this condition that had contributed to Abimelech's willingness to be liberal with Abraham. The fact of God's favor toward Abraham, in spite of Abraham's sin, should not be missed. He was the one who had been wrong from the first, in being false with Abimelech, and still God saw to it that Abraham received blessing while Abimelech experienced punishment, at least for a time. Abraham's past faithfulness to God must be credited with prompting this gracious response toward him, for his conduct before Abimelech in itself called for reprimand.

For Further Study

1. In a Bible dictionary or encyclopedia (see bibliography) read articles on: circumcision, angel, angel of the LORD, Lot, Gerar, Abimelech.
2. Do you see any significance in the fact that God changed the names of Abraham and Sarah just before the birth of Isaac? Explain your answer.
3. Why did God want all of Abraham's household circumcised, both servants and immediate family?

4. Try to characterize the full thinking of Abraham as he interceded before the Angel for Sodom.

5. Try to characterize the thinking of Lot, as he had been living in Sodom where he knew he should not be.

6. What kind of a picture does the story give concerning Sodom?

7. Make a list of comparisons and contrasts between Lot and Abraham.

Chapter 8

Abraham (III)

(Genesis 21:1 — 25:18)

The birth of Isaac must have been a highlight moment in Abraham's life. He and Sarah had of course hoped for a son all their married life, and God had finally promised that they would even have a nation-sized progeny develop from such a son. Now, at last, the son was born. Twenty-five years had elapsed since God's first promise, but these long years would have made the fulfillment all the more important when it came.

A. Birth of Isaac (Gen. 21:1-34)

With the exception of an occasional interlude, the story of Abraham from this point on relates to Isaac. He, being the son of promise, becomes the center of interest for Abraham and for the sacred record.

1. *The birth proper (Gen. 21:1-8)*

According to the twice-given promise to Abraham and Sarah, Sarah bore a son in the designated time. The parents named him Isaac, as they had been instructed (Gen. 17:19). Properly, also, they circumcised him on his eighth day. Abraham was 100 years old at the time, meaning that truly twenty-five years had elapsed since he had entered Canaan, with the first promise given (Gen. 12:4). Sarah, at the time of the birth, now laughed in a different sense than she had at the time of the promise (see Gen. 18:11-15). Then she had laughed in unbelief, but now she laughed in joy (Gen. 21:6), marveling that she should have a child in her old age. It was a happy day for both of the aged parents.

2. *Conflict with Ishmael (Gen. 21:9-21)*

Ishmael, now fourteen years old (Gen. 16:16), observed the

feasting for the young Isaac and somehow made mockery of it. He likely was jealous, for now he was no longer the heir of Abraham. The law of the day was that the son of a wife took precedence over the son of a mere handmaid, even if he was born later (as made clear from Nuzi tablets). Thus, Abraham now had known three possible heirs: first Eliezer, his servant, then Ishmael born to Hagar, and now the final and true one, Isaac.

Sarah was provoked at Ishmael's action and once more wanted to have Hagar, along with her son, expelled from the household. Abraham was hesitant to do this, for the matter was not right nor was it in accord with the custom of the day. Both from Nuzi tablets and from the Code of Hammurabi it is known that the son of a handmaid was not to be put out of a home, if a son of the wife should be born. The right of heirship would change, but not the right of home provision.

In this instance, however, God Himself assured Abraham that this expulsion was divinely approved (v. 12), and then Abraham did as Sarah wanted. He made sure, however, that Hagar had a supply of water and bread when she left. Hagar and Ishmael did leave and then wandered in the region of Beersheba until the water and bread were all gone. Then the two lay down expecting to die. The translation, "she cast the child under one of the shrubs" (v. 15) can only mean — in view of Ishmael's being fourteen — that Hagar left him lying under one shrub, where he probably was fast asleep, while she sought out shade under another where she could not witness his death.

At this point God displayed His gracious concern for the two, certainly having had this in mind when He gave Abraham permission for expulsion. An "angel of God" called out to Hagar from "heaven" to reassure her and show her a "well of water" nearby to replenish their water supply. Both mother and son were thus spared, and verses 2 and 21 imply that God continued to provide for them in days to come. Ishmael came to live in the area of Paran (south of Beersheba, a desert area) and Hagar arranged a marriage for him with a girl from Egypt. His descendants became the nation of the Ishmaelites, according to God's promise (v. 13).

3. *An interlude with Abimelech (Gen. 21:22-34)*

Now comes one of the interludes in the continuing story of Isaac. It concerns an occasion when Abimelech of Gerar visited Abraham in Beersheba. Abimelech was the king whom Abraham had earlier deceived, in respect to Sarah, but now he came to Abraham simply to assure himself of Abraham's favor. He apparently recognized Abraham as a wealthy, influential resident of a land to which he laid claim and he wanted to cultivate a good relationship. He came with his "chief captain" Phichol, no doubt to impress Abraham with his sincerity in the visit.

Abraham received him favorably, but then indicated that he had a complaint to register. Abimelech's people had seized a "well of water" that belonged to Abraham. Wells were extremely important in the dry region of the south. Abimelech responded that this was not of his doing or approval, implying that he would see to it that the matter was made right. Then Abraham agreed to a treaty with him, presenting "sheep and oxen" as tokens to the king. He also set aside "seven ewe lambs" as a witness that the disputed well did belong to himself, and, when Abimelech accepted them, he indicated by that acceptance that he agreed. The locality was now given its name "Beersheba," meaning both "a well of swearing" and "a well of the seven." With the agreement concluded, Abimelech returned to Gerar.

Abraham now planted a tamarisk tree (mistranslated "grove" in KJV) at Beersheba and called on "the LORD, the everlasting God." The reason for this indication is to signify that Abraham at the time was conscious of God's continued blessing on him and wanted to show his appreciation. The indication of verse 34 that Abraham continued to live "in the Philistines' land many days" does not mean that he moved, but that the Philistines, of whom Abimelech was king, considered the land as far east as Beersheba as belonging to them.

In passing, it may be noted that these Philistines were early predecessors of the later great influx of Philistines who came in the early twelfth century. Those who came to oppress Israel so severely in the days of Samson, Samuel, and Saul were mainly the new migrants. But they had been preceded by earlier ancestors, who apparently had come to southern Canaan from Caphor (Crete, see Jer. 47:4; Amos 9:7) some years before and here had this contact with Abraham (see Gen. 26:1, 14, 15; Exod. 13:17).

It is in order also to observe that Abraham was careful in his business relationships. He did not take advantage of others but was careful to observe the proprieties of the day in making agreements according to accepted custom. In this he provides a good example.

B. The offering of Isaac (Gen. 22:1-24)

The next main episode involving Isaac was God's directive to Abraham that he offer him in sacrifice. This must have been terribly hard for the aged man to understand, in view of the extended period in waiting for his son. But the whole occasion was for the purpose of testing the faith of this great man of God.

1. *God's directive (Gen. 22:1, 2)*

God came to Abraham when Isaac was probably about ten years old, and instructed him to take this son, indeed this son whom he loved, and go to "the land of Moriah" and sacrifice him. This Moriah was likely the place where later Solomon built the temple (2 Chron. 1:3). The indication is that God thus did "tempt" (better, "test," Heb. *nasah*) Abraham. God knew that for Abraham to be willing to offer this son, who meant so much to him, would be the highest evidence of Abraham's devotion and dedication.

2. *Abraham's obedience (Gen. 22:3-10)*

In spite of how hard the matter was, Abraham set about to do as God commanded. The next morning he began the journey to the appointed place, taking Isaac and two servants with him, as well as wood for the sacrifice. The distance he had to travel was about fifty miles and he arrived on the third day after leaving. He clearly had not hurried to get there, which is altogether understandable. Along the way he may have wanted to give God all the time possible to reveal offsetting orders, if God could possibly find this appropriate.

Leaving the two servants with the animals at the foot of Mount Moriah, Abraham and Isaac alone climbed to the top. On the way up Isaac asked his father where the "lamb for a burnt-offering" was, which shows that Abraham had not yet told the boy all that God had said. Abraham responded that God would Himself provide (Heb., "see to Himself") a lamb, possibly implying that he did yet really believe that God would require Isaac to be that one. At the top of the mountain, however, with no offsetting order revealed, Abraham then took Isaac and bound him and laid him on the altar he had built. He even raised his knife to slay the boy, before God finally stopped him. Hebrews 11:19 states that, by the time of this action, Abraham had come to believe that God would actually "raise him up" again. This surely was an outstanding expression of faith and obedience on Abraham's part.

3. *God's substitutionary provision (Gen. 22:11-14)*

Abraham was stopped when the "angel of the LORD" called from heaven, saying that Isaac need not be slain after all, because Abraham had now demonstrated the level of obedience God desired. God, of course, had not wanted the life of Isaac; He had desired only an obedience from Abraham that was willing to give that life. Abraham was now directed to a "ram" caught in a nearby thicket, and he sacrificed this animal in place of Isaac. In this lay a significant picture of the perfect Substitute that God would provide for sinful man. This Substitute would be Jesus Christ, God's own Son in human form. Because He would die in man's place, man would not have to die, providing he put his faith in this supreme Substitute.

Abraham now named the location "Jehovah-jireh," meaning "Jehovah [*Yahweh*] sees." The implication of the name is that for God to "see" a need is for Him to provide for it.

4. *The promises once more confirmed (Gen. 22:15-19)*

While Abraham was still on the top of the mountain, the "angel of the LORD" further called from heaven, this time to state the substance of the blessings that had been given several times before. God apparently saw the time appropriate to reassure Abraham that the recent directive regarding Isaac had in no way changed the plan stated before. The Angel declared that because Abraham had demonstrated this fine degree of obedience, God would truly continue to bless him and grant the large posterity promised earlier, making his "seed" as the "stars of the heaven" and as "the sand which is upon the sea shore." All nations would be blessed because of this people. No doubt Abraham was reassured by these words, human as he was, and he then returned to Beersheba with Isaac and the two servants. The fact of God's recognition of, and interest in, the human need of one of His children should not be missed.

5. *The family of Nahor (Gen. 22:20-24)*

Another interlude is now presented, though a close relation to the Abrahamic-Isaac story is apparent. The family of Nahor, brother of Abraham, who apparently had sometime earlier moved to Haran, is introduced; and the relation is that it was from this family that Isaac soon would receive a bride. News reached Abraham at this time, by some unrevealed manner, concerning these relatives (v. 20). He was told that eight sons, here all listed, had been born to Nahor and Milcah, among whom was Bethuel. To Bethuel, in turn, Rebekah (as well as Laban, though not here named) had been born, and she was to become Isaac's wife. Four other sons also are listed, who were born through a concubine named Reumah, to Nahor.

C. Death and burial of Sarah (Gen. 23:1-20)

1. *Sarah's death (Gen. 23:1, 2)*

At the age of 127, Sarah died. Isaac the son would have been thirty-seven years old at the time (cf. Gen. 17:17) and Abraham 147, with perhaps twenty-seven years having elapsed since the episode of the preceding chapter. That she died in Kirjath-arba (Hebron) means that Abraham had now moved back to Hebron from Beersheba, a distance of about thirty miles.

2. *The purchase of the cave of Machpelah (Gen. 23:3-18)*

With Sarah having died, Abraham needed a place of burial, and not owning any land of his own, he initiated efforts to buy a cave nearby which belonged to one of his Hittite friends, Ephron. At first the Hittite community urged Abraham simply to use one of their "sepulchres," but Abraham insisted that he purchase his own. Then Ephron wanted Abraham to buy the entire field, where the cave of Machpelah was found, rather than merely the cave (v. 11). The reason for this may be linked to a law among the Hittites that certain feudal services were required of those who owned property. So, if Abraham was to buy any of Ephron's property he evidently wanted him to buy all, so that such services might no longer be his obligation.

At first Ephron politely offered to give Abraham the field, but when Abraham declared that he would pay for it, he casually suggested the price of "four hundred shekels," which really was high. Abraham, however, paid it, being able to afford the price, as no doubt Ephron knew. The transaction was made properly, in the presence of the Hittite leaders, with the borders of the field carefully specified and even the trees counted. Again Abraham illustrates the propriety of doing business honestly and correctly, even though he was surely aware that he was being charged a high price for his purchase. His testimony was worth more than the extra cost involved.

3. *Burial of Sarah (Gen. 23:19, 20)*

Now Abraham buried Sarah in the cave. It was called the "cave of Machpelah," probably because the area went by that name (v. 17). Later Abraham himself was buried there (Gen.

25:9), and later still Isaac, Rebekah, and Leah (Gen. 49:31), and finally Jacob who was returned there from Egypt (Gen. 50:13). Today a large mosque stands over the traditional site containing monuments to all these.

D. A bride for Isaac (Gen. 24:1-67)

The story continues with the next big step in Isaac's life, his marriage. He was now forty years old.

1. *Abraham sends his servant to procure a bride for Isaac (Gen. 24:1-9)*

When Abraham was 140 (cf. Gen. 25:20 and 21:5), not knowing he was to live yet another thirty-five years (see Gen. 25:7), he instructed his "eldest servant" (possibly Eliezer, though he would have been old by this time) to find a wife for Isaac among the relatives he had learned were living in the Haran area. It was not fitting nor pleasing to God that a marriage occur with a Canaanite bride, for Abraham's posterity was to remain distinct.

The servant gave his oath-promise that he would do so, using the appropriate sign of placing his hand under Abraham's "thigh" or hip. This bodily area, often translated "loins," was considered the seat of the procreative powers of man (see Gen. 46:26), which made this sign appropriate in this instance (as later in Gen. 47:29); it would be through the bride to be sought that Abraham and Isaac's posterity would be propogated. When the servant had given his oath, Abraham made clear the fact that, should the bride chosen refuse to come with the servant, the servant would be free from its binding effect.

2. *The servant finds Rebekah (Gen. 24:10-27)*

With ten camels and materials for gifts, the servant set out for "the city of Nahor." Whether this was a city by this name, or whether the name is only an indication of the city where Nahor lived, is not clear. At least it was in the area of (if not identical with) Haran, where Abraham had stopped years before (see Gen. 27:43).

Arriving at the gate of the city, where the local well was located, the servant prayed to God that He would show him the bride of God's own choice and do so by having that one come out from the city and offer water both to himself and camels. Even as he finished speaking, out came Rebekah, granddaughter of Nahor, and she indeed did just as he had prescribed. The words of the servant had been well calculated, for a person who would do so much for a stranger would show herself both courteous and industrious, two prime qualities for a good wife. Rebekah was also "very fair to look upon." The servant watched and at first found the matter hard to believe that God had answered his prayer so quickly. He gave her a gift of a gold earring and two bracelets when she had finished with her watering chore, but perhaps, only in return for her kindness. When she told him her identity, however, that she was truly a granddaughter of Nahor, he became convinced that she was the one intended for Isaac.

3. *The servant and Rebekah's family (Gen. 24:28-61)*

At this, Rebekah left the servant and ran quickly to her house to report the servant's presence. Laban, her brother, immediately went out to the servant and invited him into the city and to the household. Gracious hospitality, including the provision of food, was shown to him and his company (v. 32), but the servant insisted on telling his "errand" before he would eat. Then he related the fact that he was a servant to Abraham, who was now wealthy, and that he had come the many miles to find a bride for Abraham's son, since no Canaanite girl was acceptable. He also told of the test he had proposed to God and how Rebekah had met it exactly. He closed by asking them if they would permit her to go with him as the intended bride.

The answer was that the matter was too clearly "from the LORD" for them really to have anything to say in the matter. Both Laban the brother and Bethuel the father took part in this answer, which was according to custom (cf. Gen. 34:5, 11). That Nahor is not mentioned implies that he no longer lived. At this, the servant brought forth abundant gifts for Rebekah, as well as for her brother and mother. Then all ate together and the servant stayed for the night.

In the morning he wanted to leave for home. Laban and his mother protested, asking the servant to stay at least ten days, but he insisted. They turned to Rebekah to ask if she was willing to go, and she said she was. So the servant and his men took Rebekah and left, with Rebekah receiving a parting blessing from her family.

4. *The meeting with Isaac (Gen. 24:62-67)*

Rebekah first saw her husband-to-be as he came out in the evening to meditate. The servant and Rebekah were then drawing near, and he told her who Isaac was. She covered her face with a veil in preparation for the meeting. The servant informed Isaac of how God had led him in finding Rebekah, and then Isaac took Rebekah to his mother's tent, where he made her his wife according to custom. The text adds that she filled the void in his life left by the death of Sarah.

The whole story sets forth one of the fine illustrations in Scripture of God's providential guidance for one who trusts Him. This servant went on a mission, in no way knowing how he would find the proper and suitable bride for Isaac, but, trusting God, he found her. God led him to the one and brought about His own perfect will.

E. The last days of Abraham (Gen. 25:1-18)

1. *Marriage to Keturah (Gen. 25:1-6)*

At some undesignated time in Abraham's later days, he married Keturah. It is not at all likely that he would have married her prior to Sarah's death (as some expositors believe), in view of his attitude toward having children by Hagar even when urged by his wife. Keturah is called a "concubine" here (v. 6) and in 1 Chronicles 1:32 only because she was never considered by Abraham really to fill the place of Sarah. Keturah bore Abraham six sons. Evidently the rejuvenated powers of Abraham, given in respect to Isaac's birth, yet continued. From one of these sons, Midian, the Midianite nation descended, which came to be one of Israel's later enemies (Judg. 6:2, 3, etc.). From another, Shuah, probably came one of Job's friends, Bildad the Shuhite (Job 2:11).

None of these six inherited in parallel with Isaac. They helped fulfill the promise to Abraham, that he would become the father of "nations" (plural), but he left his wealth to Isaac, only giving "gifts" to the six half brothers, whom he then sent away from his home eastward.

2. *The death of Abraham (Gen. 25:7-11)*

Abraham's death is now recorded, and it came in his 175th year, described in the text as "a good old age." By this point in history, the average length of life for man had decreased greatly from earlier time, and this age of Abraham was clearly unusual and an evidence of God's special blessing.

Abraham was buried in the cave of Machpelah, which he had purchased for Sarah, by his two sons, Isaac and Ishmael. Apparently, the six sons of Keturah either were not interested or else were too far away to have a part. The note is added that, after Abraham's death, "God blessed his son Isaac," as Isaac continued to live near the "well Lahai-roi," at Beersheba. The thought behind this mention is that, just because Abraham had died, God did not cease His blessing. Abraham's posterity was important to God, as the nation of Israel was anticipated, and His blessing continued on that line, here represented by Isaac.

3. *The descendants of Ishmael (Gen. 25:12-18)*

A last matter set forth, still in reference to Abraham, is a listing of the descendants he had through Ishmael. His descendants through Isaac also are given, immediately following, but since Isaac must be considered next for himself, this listing logically falls under his consideration. The logic of giving Ishmael's line is to show that God did as He promised in granting this first son of Abraham a large posterity (Gen. 21:18).

Twelve sons are listed for Ishmael. Some possible identifications can be made. Nebaioth probably gave his name to the Nabataeans, who developed the famous city of Petra as their capital. Tema may have given his name to the Arabian city of Tema, well known in later years as a trade center between Yemen and Syria. Kedar is mentioned in Isaiah 60:7 in connection with Nebaioth, though nothing is known otherwise about the people. The name Dumah may be retained in the modern community of Dumat et Jeudel, a few miles north of Tema.

Ishmael lived to the age of 137. That his descendants lived between Havilah (northeast of Arabia, Gen. 1:11, 12) and Shur (just east of Egypt), means that they came to spread fully across the Arabian desert, as well as the Negev region south of Palestine.

For Further Study

1. In a Bible dictionary or encyclopedia (see bibliography), read articles on: Philistines, covenant, Moriah, Nahor, Hittites, Rebekah.
2. Why do you believe God approved the desire of Sarah that Hagar and Ishmael be driven from the family home?
3. What would you say the visit of Abimelech to Abraham meant as to the stature of Abraham in his community?
4. Try to reconstruct the thinking of Abraham as he made the journey to Moriah for the purpose of "sacrificing" his son, Isaac.
5. Why would it have been wrong for Abraham to have taken a wife for Isaac from the local Canaanites?
6. Try to reconstruct the thinking of Rebekah as she made her decision to go with the servant and become Isaac's wife.

Chapter 9

Isaac

(Genesis 25:19 — 26:35)

With Abraham dead, the text now presents Isaac as the center of interest. Isaac never matches his father either in personality or spirituality. Much less is said of him than of either Abraham or Jacob. In fact, one comes to think of Isaac more as either the son of Abraham or the father of Jacob, rather than as a person for himself. Still he is counted as one of the great father-patriarchs of the Israelite nation and must be accorded an important place in the posterity line.

A. The sons, Jacob and Esau (Gen. 25:19-34)

1. *Their birth (Gen. 25:19-26)*

Rebekkah proved to be barren, just as Sarah had been. Finally, at Isaac's entreaty for his wife, God allowed her to conceive and she bore twins. Already before birth the twins "struggled together within her," and Rebekah asked God the significance. He replied that really "two nations" were in her womb, which would prove to be different from each other. One would be stronger, and the "elder" would come to serve the "younger." So, then, a continuing conflict between the respective posterities of the twins was predicted. Because it was, a similar observation is in order as was made relative to Ishmael and Isaac. Since Esau, one of the twins, became an ancestor of the present Arabs, and Jacob, the other twin, the head of the Israelites, an aspect of this prediction is still being realized in the persistent Arab-Israeli conflict.

The first to be born was Esau, who was red and hairy. Then Jacob was born, whose hand "took hold on Esau's heel" even in birth. The name "Esau" means "hairy," and "Jacob" means "one who grasps the heel" or "supplanter." The names of both boys were predictive of their respective characters, Esau becoming a man of the outdoors, and Jacob a cunning schemer.

Isaac was sixty years old when the boys were born, meaning that he had waited twenty years after his marriage for their birth. When these sixty years are added to the twenty-five that Abraham waited for Isaac, eighty-five years emerges as the number that had elapsed since God's first promise of a great posterity to Abraham: and still only one of these two boys was to be an official part of that posterity. It is evident that God did not see reason for hurry in the fulfillment of the promise. One of the hardest lessons for the Christian to learn in any day is to wait on God for the time God sees right to bring aspects of His work to reality.

2. *Esau sells his birthright to Jacob (Gen. 25:27-34)*

As the boys grew, their different dispositions became manifest. Esau loved hunting and the outdoors, while Jacob enjoyed the comforts of home. Also, Isaac came to favor the older Esau and Rebekah the younger Jacob.

One day when Esau came in from hunting, he was hungry and wanted some of the food Jacob was cooking. Jacob said he would give him some providing Esau assigned to him his birthright. The birthright belonged to Esau because, though the two were twins, he had been born first. It is clear that Jacob had coveted that right, for it gave Esau twice the inheritance of Jacob (Deut. 21:17) and also the higher blessing of the father (see Gen. 27:35). Esau foolishly reasoned that, if he now died of hunger, the birthright would do him no good anyhow, and therefore made the agreement. Jacob insisted that he swear to his decision and then gave him the food.

In this action, Jacob is to receive some blame, but the Scriptures place more on Esau when it says that, by this action, "Esau despised his birthright." The story implies that the boys had talked about this birthright prior to this, with Esau having shown enough disinterest in it to prompt Jacob here to speak as he did. He hardly would have tried for such a one-sided "bargain" unless he had reason from the past to think it would work. One cannot condone Jacob's method of procuring the honored right, but one must be even more critical of Esau for valuing it so lightly that he was willing to sell the "permanent" for a moment of enjoyment.

B. Isaac and Abimelech (Gen. 26:1-33)

The land of Palestine has periodically known famine. One famine occurred when Abraham first arrived there (Gen. 12:10), and now another was experienced by Isaac. He reacted similarly to his father in wanting to leave the area, and this brought about an appearance of God to him.

1. *God appears to Isaac (Gen. 26:1-5)*

The main instruction God now gave to Isaac was that he was not to go down into Egypt, as his father had done and as he had thought to do, but to remain in southern Canaan. God promised him that He would care for him there and effect all the promises given earlier to Abraham, referring both to the large posterity and the land itself.

2. *Isaac's falsehood regarding Rebekah (Gen. 26:6-15)*

As a result Isaac changed his mind concerning Egypt, and went instead westward to Gerar, another place his father had gone at one time. On arrival, he followed his father's example further in presenting Rebekah as his sister rather than his wife. He did this for the same reason as his father, fearing that otherwise he might be killed by the Philistines of Gerar as a way of procuring Rebekah for themselves. Rebekah was not taken, however, as Sarah had not been, but still Isaac's falsehood came to light when King Abimelech (a dynastic name, apparently, see Gen. 20:2, etc.) saw him acting as a husband, rather than a brother, toward Rebekah (v. 8).

Abimelech's response was to rebuke Isaac and then charge all his people not to harm Rebekah or consider her in any way other than another man's wife, with the penalty of death laid down for those who might disobey. Abimelech graciously permitted Isaac to remain in his land, however, which Isaac did. In spite of his sin, he was greatly prospered by God, enjoying fine crops and large flocks, to the envy of his Philistine neighbors.

It is clear that Isaac was a man strongly influenced by his father, and, disappointingly, seems to have been affected more by Abraham's weaknesses than his strong points. It would be fine if he could be found performing great acts of faith like his father, but he is not so portrayed. Rather, he is depicted running when a famine struck and then telling a falsehood to save his own life. It is noteworthy, however, that God still protected and provided for him. Surely God was gracious toward an undeserving child.

3. *A dispute over wells of water (Gen. 26:16-33)*

Because of Philistine jealousy, which apparently continued to grow, Abimelech finally asked Isaac to leave his country. Isaac did move but went only as far as "the valley of Gerar," which was hardly as far as Abimelech had intended. The Gerar region was comparatively near the Mediterranean Sea, where farming conditions better than at Beersheba normally prevail, and it is clear that Isaac was reluctant to leave.

Not having left the region, Isaac now became involved in a dispute over wells of water. The Philistines had stopped up wells that Abraham long before had dug, and Isaac now reopened these so that his large flocks and herds might have water. In doing this, Isaac's servants discovered a new "well of springing water" (natural flowing well), which was especially valuable and unusual to that part of the country. Immediately, strife with the local inhabitants developed over it, for they claimed that it belonged to them. Isaac named the well "Esek" (meaning, "strife") as a result. A second well dug nearby produced strife also, and this one Isaac named "sitnah" (meaning, "animosity"). A third well, however, dug further away from Gerar did not result in difficulty, and Isaac appropriately called it "Rehoboth" (meaning, "room").

Sometime after this, Isaac moved back to Beersheba. Apparently he believed that the famine had sufficiently abated so that he could sustain himself adequately there. When he did so, God appeared to him once more, this time by night, and assured him further of His presence and blessing. Isaac then appropriately built an altar to worship God, and also the servants dug another well.

At this point, Abimelech came from Gerar to Beersheba to make a treaty with Isaac, much as had been done earlier with Abraham. The reason was apparently the same; Abimelech recognized the powerful influence of Isaac and his wealth in the country, and he wanted to be assured of his good will. He came with two of his leading men, one again named Phichol (cf. Gen. 21:22, possibly the same man as in Abraham's day) and one with the name Ahuzzath. The treaty Abimelech sought was essentially the same as that made with Abraham. Isaac's agreement was signified by a feast he prepared.

When these visitors had departed, Isaac's servants came to announce the discovery of another fine well, which Isaac named "Shebah (meaning, "oath"). Isaac now, once more (like his father) named the locality Beersheba, this time primarily because of the idea, "oath," rather than "seven." (As explained at the time Abraham first gave the name Beersheba to the place, Gen. 21:31, the name means both the "well of the oath" and "well of the seven.")

C. Esau's marriages (Gen. 26:34, 35)

At the age of forty, Esau married two Hittite women, Judith and Bashemath. This was contrary to God's will, if Abraham's posterity was to remain distinct from native peoples. The matter was a cause for concern on the part of Isaac and Rebekah. That Esau was willing to do this shows that he had a rebellious nature, ready to do what he desired no matter what his parents thought.

For Further Study

1. In a Bible dictionary or encyclopedia (see bibliography) read articles on: Isaac, Esau, well, Beersheba.
2. What do you think was the cause of the excessive influence Abraham had on Isaac?
3. Make a list of the good points in Isaac's life and a list of the bad points. In view of your list, what conclusions would you make regarding Isaac as a person?
4. How would you characterize Esau as a person?
5. Reconstruct the thinking of the Gerar populace regarding Isaac, during the time he stayed in their country.
6. Was Isaac right in letting the Philistines have the wells of water he dug, or should he have fought for them?

Chapter 10

Jacob (I)

(Genesis 27:1 — 30:43)

The sacred record has much to say about Jacob also. He is shown to have been a vigorous person, much in the pattern of Abraham. He did not reach the spiritual stature of his grandfather, however. He had a weakness for scheming but he had some strong points in his life as well. It was with him, finally, that God began to produce a sizable posterity.

A. The blessing by Isaac (Gen. 27:1-46)

1. *The decision of Isaac to bless Esau (Gen. 27:1-5)*

It was a patriachal custom for an aged father to grant a blessing on his children prior to death. Isaac was now getting old, with his eyesight rapidly failing, and he decided to bestow this blessing. Because Esau was his eldest, and he favored him over Jacob anyhow (Gen. 25:28), he chose to grant his highest blessing on Esau and informed him of his intent. He told Esau to go hunting for a deer and prepare him a venison dish, at which time he would bestow the blessing. Rebekah overheard the conversation, however, and while Esau went to get the venison, she schemed with her favored son, Jacob, how he might procure the blessing instead. Nothing is said in the text whether or not either Isaac or Rebekah knew of the prior sale by Esau of his birthright to Jacob, but actually, because of that sale, Esau had no right to this favor of his father.

2. *Rebekah and Jacob plot to deceive (Gen. 27:6-17)*

At first Jacob objected to the idea of trying to deceive his father, but Rebekah persuaded him to try. Jacob wanted the blessing, all right, but he was fearful that his mother's plan might not work.

Finally he consented. Rebekah made "savory meat" from a goat, so that Jacob might bring this to Isaac, in place of the venison dish that Esau was intending to prepare. Then she put the skin of the slain goat on Jacob's hands and neck, to make him feel hairy like Esau, in case his father would want to touch him. She even took some of Esau's clothes in which to dress Jacob, knowing that Isaac would have to depend on his sense of touch and smell for identification, since he could no longer see well. Thus equipped, Jacob presented himself before Isaac as if he were Esau.

Though Jacob surely was wrong in thus agreeing to a scheme to deceive his father, two matters should be kept in mind which mitigate against criticizing him too severely. One is that the blessing really did belong to him, since Esau had sold him the birthright, and the other is that the idea of the deception was born by Rebekah, not Jacob. It may be added that for either Rebekah or Jacob to have even thought of deceiving Isaac provides a significant commentary on Isaac as a husband and father. Surely he had not been the strong and loving leader of the family he should have been, so that a proper respect had been earned by him. One cannot think of Sarah and Isaac, for instance, ever having contrived to deceive Abraham.

3. *The blessing bestowed on Jacob (Gen. 27:18-29)*

When Jacob presented himself to Isaac, the old man immediately wanted to make sure of the identity of the one before him. He evidently was suspicious from the first, due especially to the sound of Jacob's voice (v. 22). His initial question concerned the brevity of time in which the meat had been procured, and then he wanted to feel Jacob's skin just as Rebekah had foreseen. The feel of the skin and the smell of Esau's clothes convinced him that everything was all right, and so he proceeded with eating of the "savory meat" that Rebekah had prepared. Then he bid Jacob kiss him, so that he could smell him at still closer range, and this too satisfied him. He then felt he could safely bestow the blessing.

The blessing consisted of his wish that his son be prospered by God, that people in general render him service, including other sons of his mother, and that all who cursed him should be cursed and those who blessed him should be blessed. By these words, Isaac clearly was intending that Esau be the one through whom the covenantal line, started from Abraham, should continue. But in this he was going directly against the will of God. God had told Rebekah, at the birth of the twins, that the elder should serve the younger, and certainly Isaac knew about this. So, then, though Rebekah was wrong in making this plot, and Jacob was wrong in agreeing to carry it out, Isaac also was wrong in trying to circumvent God's directive.

4. *The remorse of Esau (Gen. 27:30-41)*

Jacob had just left Isaac's presence when Esau came in with the "savory meat" he had prepared from his procured venison. Inquiry quickly made Isaac realize that this was indeed Esau and that he had been tricked by Jacob. He was shaken emotionally, for he had tried to be so careful in his identification with Jacob, but he had to tell Esau that the blessing given would still hold true for his brother, though trickery had been employed to get it. Esau now cried out in despair at having been "supplanted" by Jacob these "two times" (v. 36), and asked if there was not at least some blessing that Isaac could bestow on him. Finally, Isaac did wish for him that he too would experience prosperity at God's hand, though he would have to be servant to his brother; he said, further, that Esau would live "by the sword" (i.e. by fighting) and that by this means he would occasionally break Jacob's yoke from off his neck.

In respect to these last words, it is significant to notice later history. The Edomites, the people who descended from Esau, fought with Israel many times, with the result that they were freed from Israelite control on several of these occasions (see 2 Chron. 21:8-10; 28:16, 17).

The result of Esau's great disappointment was that he now came to hate Jacob, and he determined to have his life as soon as his father died (v. 41). At the moment, it seemed that this time might not be far away, but in actual fact Isaac continued to live for another forty-three years.[1]

5. *The reaction of Rebekah (Gen. 27:42-46)*

Not only did Jacob's action bring bitterness to Esau, but it also made an unpleasant situation for Rebekah. Learning of Esau's threat, she had to counsel Jacob to leave home. Jacob was her favorite, which means this would not have been easy. She told Jacob to flee to her brother Laban, in her old home area of Haran. She spoke of Jacob staying there a "few days," but it actually proved to be twenty years. No indication is given when Rebekah died, but she may not have seen Jacob again. She spoke not only to

[1] For discussion of this figure, see Keil & Delitzsch, *Commentary on the Pentateuch,* I, pp. 273, 274.

Jacob of the matter but also to Isaac, giving the reason to him that Jacob should not "take a wife of the daughters of Heth" as Esau had done (v. 46). In other words, Jacob should procure a wife in Haran among relatives, as Isaac himself had done.

B. Jacob's journey to Haran (Gen. 28:1-22)

1. *The departure (Gen. 28:1-5)*

Isaac was not so provoked with either Jacob or Rebekah that he would not cooperate with his wife in giving counsel to his son, and he now summoned Jacob and told him to leave home and go to Haran to find a wife. Sometimes liberal expositors have imagined a conflict in the story here, asserting that it presents two different reasons for Jacob's departure for Haran: one, to escape Essau; and, two, to get a wife. There is no conflict, however, for Jacob went for both reasons. Having to leave home because of Esau's anger, it was well that he go to Haran where he might at the same time find a wife. The region is here called "Padan-aram" (meaning, probably, "field of Aram"), but no question exists but that it was the Haran area, because it was Laban's home (brother of Rebekah) and it was already called by this term in 25:20, which speaks of Isaac's marriage to Rebekah.

Isaac also included words of further blessing for Jacob at this time, before sending him away, showing that he now recognized that God's line would truly be carried on through Jacob rather than Esau.

2. *An interlude regarding Esau (Gen. 28:6-9)*

An interlude regarding Esau is now inserted in the story. When Esau realized that his parents were grieved at his Hittite marriages and that accordingly they had now sent Jacob to Haran to get a wife, he seems to have tried to gain favor with them by now marrying a daughter of Ishmael named Mahalath. He apparently reasoned that, since Ishmael was related through Abraham, this marriage should be pleasing to them. He did not recognize in this, however, that Ishmael had been separated from the house of Abraham by God Himself. His intention may have been good, but he really did not improve his position any, either with his parents or with God.

3. *Jacob's dream of the ladder to heaven (Gen. 28:10-22)*

When Jacob had traveled as far as Luz (Bethel, a distance from

Beersheba of about fifty-five miles) on his way to Haran, he had a dream one night. He saw a ladder extended to heaven, with angels going up and down on it. At the top stood God Himself, who voiced words of promise to him as He earlier had to Abraham and Isaac. He said that Jacob would have a large posterity, that this land of Canaan would be given to that posterity, and then that He would be with Jacob as he now left Canaan, would prosper him while gone, and would cause him to return in due time.

When Jacob awakened, he was emotionally stirred. He said that he had not realized God was in this place, and then he took the stone, which he had used for a pillow, and poured oil on it as he named the place "Bethel" (meaning, "house of God"). He further promised that if God would indeed be with him, as God had promised in the dream, he would in turn follow Him as his God and give a "tenth" back to God of all that God gave him.

This is the first instance recorded of God revealing Himself to Jacob. The occasion was highly significant, for it let Jacob know firsthand — and not only by his father's blessing — that he was truly the one through whom God would continue the promised line from Abraham. God, being at the top of the ladder, was the One who could and would provide for Jacob, and the angels, going up and down, would be those to convey the blessings God was willing to grant. No reasons exist why we should not feel that Jacob made the vow seriously. His words show that he had not been well educated in respect to God's reality and presence before, but now that God had given these wonderful promises, he was ready to respond as best he could. The fact that he promised a "tenth" of his income to God shows again that God had set forth the principal of tithing sometime in early history (cf. Gen. 14:20).

It should be realized that Jacob was no longer young at the time of this flight to Haran, as one might think since he had not yet married. His age can be determined exactly, from figures given later in respect to the time of Joseph's birth (see Gen. 47:9; 41:46, 47, 54; 45:11; 31:41; 30:25), and these show him to have been just seventy-seven (with Isaac, then, being 137, Gen. 25:26). The husband that Leah and Rachel was to get was not what one would call a young man, then. He evidently was strong and in good health, however, as shown by the good work he would do for Laban in the next few years.

C. Jacob's marriage to Leah and Rachel (Gen. 29:1-30)

1. *Jacob's meeting with Rachel (Gen. 29:1-12)*

God brought about a meeting of Jacob with Rachel, daughter of Laban, even before Jacob entered the city of Haran. As he approached the well of the city, where sheep were watered at a particular time of the day, Rachel came to the well with her flock to wait for this time, along with others already there. When Jacob learned that she was Laban's daughter, he took it upon himself to roll the stone cover off from the capped well immediately, and then he watered her flock as well as those of the others waiting. This done, Jacob informed Rachel of his blood relationship to her as first cousin, and she quickly ran to tell her father Laban, Jacob's uncle.

2. *The double marriage (Gen. 29:13-30)*

Laban now went out to meet Jacob, naturally eager to see the son of his sister and to learn about her, who had left home some ninety-seven years before (Jacob here being seventy-seven and born twenty years after Rebekah married Isaac). Jacob moved into the house, remained one month, and then an agreement was made between Laban and Jacob that Jacob should work seven years for him that he might have Rachel, his daughter, as wife.

When the seven years were completed, a marriage took place, but Laban tricked Jacob by veiling an older sister, Leah — who was not as attractive as Rachel — and presenting her to Jacob instead of Rachel. Jacob had been given to scheme and trickery with Esau and Isaac, but he here met his match and more with Laban. Laban explained that the custom of the country was that the older sister should be married first. He went on to say that, if Jacob still wanted Rachel, he would have to work another seven years. Certainly this was trickery of the most provoking kind, but Jacob agreed, due to his love for Rachel, and labored, then, a total of fourteen years for both wives. When one considers the time of birth of resulting children, however, it is evident that the marriage to both daughters took place at about the same time (one week apart, v. 27), meaning that Jacob worked out the seven years for Rachel after the marriage. To both daughters, Laban gave a personal handmaid; to Leah he gave Zilpah, and to Rachel, Bilhah.

D. The birth of Jacob's sons (Gen. 29:31-30:24)

Notice was made earlier that eighty-five years elapsed, following

God's first promise to Abraham of a large posterity, before Jacob and Esau were born. Now an additional seventy-seven years, plus the seven of Jacob's service, passed before Jacob was even married, for a total of 169 years. At this time, however, a total of twelve sons came to be born in the next few years. They were born to his two wives and also to their two handmaids. One cannot condone Jacob having children by the handmaids, but in so doing he was following a custom of the day, even as Abraham had with Hagar.

Because Jacob loved Leah less than Rachel, God saw fit to give children to Leah first, while Rachel remained barren. Four sons were born to her and Rachel, in desperation, gave Bilhah to Jacob that he bear sons through her. Leah then retaliated by giving Zilpah, her handmaid, to Jacob. Two sons were born to each of these servants. After this, Leah herself bore two more sons and then finally Rachel was permitted to bear and she gave Jacob two sons, though the second, Benjamin, was not born until the family had returned to Canaan. Daughters too were born at some time (Gen. 37:35), but only one of these is mentioned by name, Dinah, born to Leah (Gen. 30:21). Stress is placed on the sons, according to the custom of the day. A chart of their births, in order of listing, appears as follows:

MOTHER	SON	MEANING OF NAME
Leah	Reuben	See, a son. "The LORD hath looked."
	Simeon	Hearing. "The LORD hath heard."
	Levi	Joining. "My husband will be joined unto me."
	Judah	Praise. "Now will I praise the LORD."
Bilhah	Dan	Judge. "God hath judged me."
	Naphtali	Wrestling. "With great wrestlings have I wrestled with my sister."
Zilpah	Gad	Troop. "A troop cometh."
	Asher	Gladness. "Happy am I."
Leah	Issachar	He brings wages. "God hath given me my hire."
	Zebulun	Dwelling. "Now will my husband dwell with me."

	Joseph	Adding. "The Lord shall add to me another son."
Rachel		
	Benjamin (Gen. 35:18)	Son of my right hand. Rachel, who died at the time, called him Ben-oni (son of my sorrow), but Jacob changed his name to Benjamin.

After the birth of Asher by Zilpah, Reuben (about four years old), son of Leah, brought some "mandrakes" to his mother. This plant belongs to the potato family and has a forked torso-shaped root which apparently gave rise to the superstition that the plant carried aphrodisiac properties (for which reason its fruit is still called "love apples"). Rachel bargained with Leah for some of them, thinking that they would help her have children, but they did not. Instead, Leah had more children while Rachel remained barren. God no doubt wanted to impress Rachel that He was the One who produced fertility. Finally, however, God did give her conception and Joseph was born, and, later still, after reaching Canaan, Benjamin also was born. This made a total of twelve sons for Jacob.

From verse 25, we see that Jacob's fulfillment of his fourteen years did not occur until after Joseph's birth, so it becomes clear that all eleven of these sons were born during Jacob's second period of seven years of service. What is more, Leah herself had six of these sons. This means that the order of the births as given was not fully chronological. Probably Rachel gave Bilhah to Jacob before all four of Leah's first sons were born, and also Leah gave him Zilpah. Even both of Leah's two later sons, Issachar and Zebulun, could not have been born before Rachel became pregnant with Joseph. The order of births as set forth clearly is based on the mothers involved as well as on chronological sequence.

Notice should be made, further, that this story reveals some of the evils of polygamy. One of the worst is jealousy between wives. Both Leah and Rachel were jealous of each other, in respect both to Jacob's love and also to having children. No doubt, the children as they grew up also naturally divided themselves into mother-groupings. Jacob's household could not have been very happy as a result, and this could only have been a source of sorrow for the father.

E. Jacob's wages during six additional years (Gen. 30:25-43)

1. *The wage of agreement (Gen. 30:25-36)*

At the close of the bargained fourteen years, Jacob wanted to return to Canaan but Laban wanted him to stay, recognizing that the prosperity he had been experiencing was because of God's blessing on this son-in-law. He even allowed Jacob to set the wage agreement between them, if he would remain. The main point of the agreement was that Jacob should have all unusually colored sheep and goats that would be born (i.e., spotted ones, for normally sheep are a solid white and goats a solid black or dark brown).

Jacob also spoke of removing all that were presently of unusual color, but whether he had in mind to do this so that he could keep them and breed them as he wished (thus to his advantage) or so that Laban might take them and thus protect himself from any extra advantage for Jacob is not clear. Probably the latter is more likely, but, whatever Jacob's intention, Laban made sure of the matter by separating the spotted animals out himself and giving them under the care of his own sons. Then he sent the sons with these and other animals three days distant from Jacob, so that Jacob would have no possibility of breeding these animals to increase the offspring that would make up his wages. Laban thus showed his scheming nature once again, as over against Jacob.

2. *Jacob becomes wealthy (Gen. 30:37-43)*

In spite of Laban's efforts, however, Jacob still prospered greatly under the blessing of God. Large numbers of the multicolored animals were born, whether he had the parent stock of this kind or not.

Jacob employed natural methods to bring this manner of increase for himself, but whether God was in any way pleased to use these methods as means to bring the prosperity, or whether He gave it in spite of the methods, is not clear. Jacob did three things. He placed peeled, streaked poles before the eyes of the animals at the time of their breeding, for he believed this would provide a prenatal influence helpful to his cause (vv. 37-40); he put all the multicolored animals that were born, by themselves so that they would interbreed and hopefully produce more of their own kind (v. 40); and he made sure that the prenatal measures he employed were used in connection with the strongest of the animals, rather than the weakest, so that the multicolored, that might be born, would themselves tend to be stronger (v. 41).

Verse 43 states that Jacob increased "exceedingly" in the number of animals that were properly his, and this called for many servants to care for them. The true reason for this was simply God's blessing, in accordance with His earlier promise. That Jacob tried to improve his situation by the natural devices is blameworthy on his part. It is understandable, in view of the deceitful measures Laban had employed in respect to him, but still Jacob should have simply trusted God to provide for him as He wished.

For Further Study

1. In a Bible dictionary or encyclopedia (see bibliography) read articles on: Jacob, Laban, Leah, Padan-aram.
2. Reconstruct Isaac's thinking in wanting to bestow the main blessing on Essau, in view of God's direct word to Rebekah at the birth of the twins.
3. Reconstruct Esau's thinking when he realized he had been tricked by Jacob.
4. Reconstruct Rebekah's thinking when she realized she would have to send her favorite son, Jacob, away from home.
5. Think through Jacob's reaction at the dream he had at Bethel.
6. How would you evaluate Laban as a person?

Chapter 11

Jacob (II)

(Genesis 31:1 — 36:43)

A total of twenty years passed while Jacob was in Haran, fourteen spent in serving for his two wives and six more for wages. During these years, his family took on size and his wages resulted in an abundance of multicolored livestock. Finally he had enough of life in the foreign area and, having received God's approval, he made plans to return to Canaan.

A. Jacob leaves for Canaan (Gen. 31:1-55)

1. *The decision to leave (Gen. 31:1-16)*

When six years of this "wages" agreement had passed (v. 41), Jacob saw that the attitude of Laban was changing toward him. Laban's sons seem to have been complaining that all their inheritance was going to Jacob, in view of the unusual growth of his wealth at what they believed was their father's expense. Accordingly, when a directive from God came to return to Canaan (v. 3), it was not hard for Jacob to obey. He called his two wives out to the field (evidently to insure secrecy) to tell them of his new plans, rehearsing to them how their father had changed his wages "ten times," while God had prospered him in spite of this. Then he added that the "angel of God" had indeed given instructions for the return (vv. 11-13). On hearing these words, both Rachel and Leah voiced their approval, even saying that they too were counted as "strangers" by their father.

2. *The secret departure (Gen. 31:17-21)*

The result was that Jacob now left. He waited for doing so until Laban had gone to shear his sheep, which apparently were under the care of his sons. Then Jacob left, with the sizable company of his wives, children, servants, and livestock. Without telling Jacob, Rachel also took "the images that were her father's" (v. 19). Laban did not learn of Jacob's departure until three days later.

Jacob is to be criticized for departing in this secret manner, but once more the action is understandable. When he had been the recipient of so many times of deception by Laban, he could well have thought to avoid a difficult scene by leaving in this way. He had wanted to depart six years earlier, and his father-in-law had talked him out of it. Now there could be much wrangling over whether all that Jacob possessed really belonged to him. Conversations and disputes of this kind are never pleasant. What Jacob had was clearly his because of God's blessing on him. He was not taking animals or goods that belonged to Laban.

One exception existed to this, however, as noted. Rachel took her father's "images" without Jacob's knowledge. The reason why Rachel did this is quite clear today. "Images" *(teraphim)* of this kind symbolized the right of heirship of the oldest son. By taking them, Rachel apparently wanted assurance that Jacob would be considered in that position. Laban's other sons, who had become jealous in recent years, clearly had been born since Jacob's arrival twenty years before. Because they were actual sons of Laban, however, and not merely sons-in-law like Jacob, they now carried primacy over Jacob in this right. Rachel, evidently, did not want to accord them that right, especially in view of their attitude. In this Rachel was wrong. Jacob himself seems to have been satisfied with the possessions he had, without laying claim to more, and he had a large inheritance waiting for him back in Canaan anyway.

3. *Pursued by Laban (Gen. 31:22-55)*

As soon as Laban learned of Jacob's departure, he was angry and gave chase. Even though Jacob had three days' start, he was sure he could catch him because he could travel much faster, not having animals to drive as Jacob did. It took him seven days to do so, however, indicating that Jacob pushed along as rapidly as he could. Before making contact, Laban was warned by God in a dream by night not to harm Jacob in any way (v. 24).

Laban caught up with Jacob in "mount Gilead." Jacob therefore had nearly reached Canaan by that time. "Mount Gilead" is roughly correspondent to what often is called Transjordan, and it would have been in the northern portion, for the Jabbok had not yet been reached (see Gen. 32:22). Laban first expressed great hurt that he had not been able to bid his family a proper farewell. He may have been sincere in what he said, but surely any parting scene, had Jacob not gone secretly, would have been other than what Laban described here. That he spoke of "sons" in Jacob's group to whom he had not been able to say good-by was really a reference to "grandsons," for none of his own sons, certainly, had departed with Jacob.

Then, with preliminary remarks made, Laban came to what was of much greater import to him. Why had Jacob "stolen" his "gods"? Jacob properly professed complete innocence at the implied accusation and gave Laban full permission to search the camp as he wished. Laban did so, but did not find the images. When he came to Rachel's tent, she excused herself for not rising to greet her father, and the reason was that she had hidden the objects in the camel's saddle[1] on which she was seated.

When Laban did not find the objects, Jacob, still not knowing of Rachel's guilt showed marked provocation at his father-in-law for having made his charge and search. He also took the opportunity to voice words of complaint at the treatment he had received at Laban's hand over the prior twenty years. He spoke of his own service as having been faithful, which was for the most part true, and also of God's blessing on him in spite of Laban's having changed his wages "ten times."

Laban's only response was that all he saw about him in Jacob's camp had been his: the daughters who had become Jacob's wives, the children to whom they had given birth, and all the animals which had been produced from livestock that belonged to him. He could not say, however, that Jacob had taken any of these improperly. All had been according to agreement. As a result, Laban proposed that the two simply make a covenant never to bother each other again. Laban's main interest in this was to prevent Jacob from ever returning to lay claim to more of his property as inheritance, to which the stolen images gave him the right. Jacob was agreeable, for he in no way intended to do such a thing. Rachel probably was displeased however, since now her images were of no symbolic value. Laban thus achieved that for which he had really come, even though he did not find the images.

---

[1] Camel's "saddle" (Heb. *car*) is more accurate than camel's "furniture" (as in KJV). Rachel apparently had taken the saddle from her camel and placed it in her tent, perhaps partially as a precaution in view of the images hidden in it.

As an emblem of the covenant, the two men set up a pillar where they were. Laban called its name Jegar-sahadutha (meaning, "heap of witness" in Aramaic, which was his language), and Jacob called it Galeed (meaning the same in Hebrew). A further name, Mizpah (meaning, "watchpost") was given to it, for it signalized the pillar as a place of watching to see that neither party passed to hurt the other. That evening Jacob offered a sacrifice, after which all ate together. The next morning Laban left, speaking words of blessing on Jacob's family.

B. Jacob's encounter with Esau (Gen. 32:1-33:15)

Not only had Jacob left an unpleasant situation in Haran, which now had been dealt with, but he also had one facing him back in Canaan. Esau, who had planned to kill Jacob because of his trickery twenty years before, was still there. Jacob was understandably anxious when he thought of the inevitable meeting with this brother.

1. *Met by angels of God (Gen. 32:1, 2)*

As Jacob now moved on toward Canaan, sensing this anxiety deeply, he was met by a company of "angels of God." Nothing is indicated as to what the angels said, but the implication is that God had sent them to encourage His fearful servant. Jacob named the place of meeting Mahanaim, meaning "two camps." The one camp in view would have been this angelic group, here serving as God's camp of encouragement, and the other as his own group which needed the reassurance.

2. *Preparation to meet Esau (Gen. 32:3-23)*

Jacob now made preparations for meeting his brother. The first effort was simply to send messengers to inform Esau of his coming and to tell him something of the blessing of God on him since having left twenty years before. Jacob certainly was not moving very fast in his journey at this point, for the messengers had time to travel all the way to Edom (where Esau now lived, v. 3) and back, with the main company being about in the same place when they returned as when they left. They came back with the frightening news that Esau was actually coming to meet Jacob, and that he was accompanied by 400 men.

This prompted Jacob to do three things. He divided both people and animals into two groups, one to precede the other, thinking that if Esau came on one, at least the other could escape. Then he did the most important thing of all in going to God in prayer about his problem (vv. 9-12). He reminded God of His earlier promise to him, confessed his personal unworthiness of any consideration by God, and closed by asking that God be gracious in delivering him from the impending danger. Third, he made up a present for his brother, apparently thinking thus to assuage his supposed bitterness. The gift consisted of 580 animals: goats, sheep, camels, cattle, and asses. These he divided into three droves, so that Essau would meet one gift-group after the other, apparently to increase the impression of the total gift. These gift-groups were to precede, evidently, both of the two main divisions of the total company.

With these matters carried out, Jacob sent all across the Jabbok River the following evening, with respective instructions, and then he remained alone on the north side, apparently to think further and to sleep if he could.

3. *Wrestling with the Angel of the Lord (Gen. 32:24-32)*

Jacob did not sleep, however, for he suddenly found himself engaged in a wrestling match with "a man," and continued to be so until the "breaking of the day." The identification of this "man" as the Angel of the Lord is certain, both from the description given and a later commentary by Hosea (12:4,5). At some point in the physical encounter, the Angel touched Jacob's thigh so that it became impaired. The Angel then wished to be let go, but Jacob insisted that He first pronounce a blessing on his human opponent. Jacob thus indicated his own recognition of the identity of the heavenly adversary, and he wanted His blessing, particularly in view of the coming encounter with Esau.

The Angel did as requested. First, he changed Jacob's name from Jacob to "Israel," meaning, "fighter for God." This indicated that God now saw Jacob as having been changed from a "supplanter" to a "fighter," which surely was significant. Then the Angel stated that Jacob, in this capacity as "fighter," would have "power with God and with men." Jacob next asked the Angel for His name, but He did not give it (signifying, no doubt, that Jacob already really knew) but instead pronounced the "blessing" Jacob had requested, which was far more meaningful. The Angel now left Jacob, and Jacob appropriately named the place Peniel, meaning "face of God," saying, "For I have seen God face to face."

This occasion was of prime importance to Jacob. The wrestling occurred as an actual physical encounter, but it also symbolized Jacob's wrestling with God for God's blessing on his life. That the

Angel wrestled in return symbolized that God had something against Jacob in this desire, namely his sin. And that the Angel finally blessed Jacob and even changed his name shows that Jacob had now received God's approval on his life and that he could expect God's favor in still greater measure in days to come. The story implies that the hurt done to Jacob's thigh was real and permanent and was no doubt intended as a continuing reminder of this important occasion. In theological terms, this was not the time of Jacob's "conversion," but it was a significant step ahead in his "progressive sanctification."

4. *The meeting with Esau (Gen. 33:1-15)*

Significantly, it was on the day following that Jacob met his brother. God had timed the Angel encounter so that Jacob would have this fresh encouragement just before the meeting. On seeing Esau, Jacob moved forward to meet him alone, placing his family behind him in three groups: first the maids with their children, then Leah with hers, and then Rachel with Joseph. He bowed deeply before Esau, but Esau only ran forward to meet and embrace Jacob in a warm greeting. This was entirely in contrast to what Jacob had expected, and it could only have given great relief to him. After the embrace, Esau asked who all these were who were with Jacob and also what the meaning was behind the three droves of animals he had already met. Jacob explained that the people were the family with which God had blessed him and that the droves had been gifts intended for Esau.

No doubt Esau was greatly impressed, but he only protested that he had no need for such gifts, seeing he too had all he needed. At Jacob's insistence, however, he did accept them, for to have refused would have been considered an insult. Esau then suggested that the two companies journey back to his home region of Mt. Seir together, but Jacob stated that this would not be workable, since his company would have to travel too slowly, having flocks and herds to drive. He did speak of visiting Esau at some later time, however, though if he ever did no record was kept.

Jacob's statement to Esau that he saw his face as "the face of God" (v. 10) calls for a comment. Jacob probably meant by this that he saw Esau's face as one that had been changed by God. When Jacob had left twenty years before, Esau had hated him and no doubt his facial expression showed this. Now, however, his face showed love. Jacob apparently recognized that God had worked in Esau's heart during the years, taking away the bitterness. He likely saw this as one of the ways God was already carrying out the promise of the night before from the Angel.

C. Back in Canaan (Gen. 33:16-35:29)

Esau now returned south to Edom, but Jacob, whatever his intentions for visiting Esau sometime, turned west to go across the Jordan and into Canaan. He stopped for a time at Succoth, still in Transjordan but about five miles west of Penuel,[2] and then moved on into the land proper.

1. *Jacob stops at Shechem (Gen. 33:16-20)*

Jacob's course, as he crossed the Jordan, continued almost straight westward, because his first major stop was at Shechem. This was the place where Abraham had first stopped years before when he had initially entered Canaan. Jacob apparently planned to stay here for some time, because he even purchased property from Hamor, a citizen of Shechem, and built an altar there. It was no doubt due to this purchase that he could later give land here to Joseph, as indicated in John 4:5. He named the altar he built, El-elohe-Israel, meaning "God, the God of Israel." The name "Israel" would be used here in the sense of Jacob's new name, which suggests that, by this name of the altar, Jacob wished to testify to his neighbors that God was truly his God.

2. *A sad episode with the Shechemites (Gen. 34:1-31)*

Jacob's plan for remaining at Shechem suddenly was interrupted by a sad episode of sin. Sin regularly breeds more sin, and it did here.

Dinah, daughter of Leah, was seduced one day by Shechem, the son of Hamor from whom Jacob had bought his property. Shechem now wanted to marry Dinah and so his father came to Jacob and his sons to make the request. He proposed, in fact, that Jacob's family continue to intermarry with the Shechemites as a normal practice. Though Shechem and Hamor were probably sincere in their offer of friendship, what they proposed was directly contrary to the will of God, who wanted distinctness for Jacob's family to be maintained. It also was contrary to the wishes of Dinah's brothers, who believed Shechem had violated their sister.

They craftily feigned interest, however, by suggesting that all

---

[2] In verse 30 this name is spelled in the Hebrew with an "i" and in verse 31 (as well as elsewhere) with a "u."

the Schechemites become circumcised like themselves, so that such intermarriage might be possible. When Hamor set this suggestion before the Shechemites, they agreed, showing that they held this man and his son in high esteem. On the third day after the circumcision was done, however, when all the men were still sore from the operation, Simeon and Levi, two of Dinah's brothers, entered the city with swords and killed all the men, including Hamor and Shechem. They found Dinah and took her away with them. After this, the other sons joined in the sacking of the city, seizing spoil and even taking wives and children captive.

Though Jacob himself had not been pleased with the defilement of his daughter by Shechem either, he had not been party to this outrageous retaliation by his sons, and now he rebuked especially Simeon and Levi who had been the worst offenders. He told them that they had made him "to stink" among the people of the area, so that now all of the family was in danger of being killed in counterretaliation. The depth to which Jacob was grieved by the occasion is revealed in his mention of it years later when bestowing his "blessings" on his sons just before his death (Gen. 49:5). Two wrongs never make a right. Shechem had been wrong in defiling Dinah, but Simeon and Levi had been wrong also in their vicious retaliation.

3. *Another experience at Bethel (Gen. 35:1-15)*

As a way of protecting Jacob, God now told the patriarch to move south to Bethel, where God had first appeared to him when he had fled from Esau. Jacob agreed, but before moving he instructed that all "strange gods" among the members of his household should be put away. Perhaps he had learned by this time concerning the images Rachel had taken, and also that some of the sons or servants possessed certain images or "charm" earrings as well. He apparently remembered the sacredness of the earlier visit to Bethel and wanted to return there as free from defilement as possible.

As the company moved, God put His "terror" (v. 5) on the neighboring populace so that no attack was made against the company, and Jacob was able to travel the twenty miles to Bethel without incident. Here he built an altar, as in Shechem, and called it El-beth-el, meaning "The God of Bethel." Then God appeared to him once more. He spoke of Jacob's change of name and repeated the same basic promises (concerning posterity and land) that He had stated earlier to him (as well as to Abraham and Isaac).

In view of this further revelation, and surely in memory of his first visit to the place, Jacob now erected a pillar, poured a liquid offering and oil on it, and named the place once more "Bethel." Apparently Jacob wanted to relive his experience here, of more than twenty years earlier, thus making the location now doubly precious to him. For the rest of his days, Bethel would stand out in his memory as a place of prime spiritual importance.

4. *Rachel dies in childbirth (Gen. 35:16-26)*

Leaving Bethel after a time, Jacob moved on south, no doubt heading for his old home area of Hebron and Beersheba. As the family neared Bethlehem on the way, however, he experienced a sad loss. Rachel gave birth to Benjamin and in so doing died. The birth of another son by this one whom Jacob loved so much would have been a great joy, but the loss of his beloved Rachel must have been a major reason for sorrow.

Just before her death, Rachel herself named the little son Ben-oni, meaning "son of my sorrow," but Jacob renamed him Benjamin, meaning "son of my right hand." The significance of the changed name was that a person's right hand was considered a place of honor. Benjamin was to have this place in respect to Jacob. Jacob did not take Rachel's body to the cave of Machpelah for burial, but instead laid it to rest where he then was and placed a monument on the grave. Still today a small building, made by the Crusaders, is said to mark the site. It appears to be too far south, however, in view of 1 Samuel 10:2 and Jeremiah 31:15 (see Matt. 2:18), which locate the grave much nearer Ramah, just north of Jerusalem.

This birth of Benjamin gave reason for a complete list of Jacob's sons to be given in the text (vv. 22-26). No new information is given regarding the sons except for one distressing note. This is that the oldest, Reuben, had relations with Bilhah, the handmaid of Rachel, perhaps taking the opportunity following Rachel's death. Reuben could hardly have been more than in his late teen years at the time, having been no more than thirteen at the time the family left Haran. The statement that Jacob "heard it" (v. 22), implies heartfelt grief at the information.

5. *Death of Isaac (Gen. 35:27-29)*

Jacob now moved on to Mamre (Hebron), where Abraham had lived for so many years and where Jacob's father, Isaac, was living at the time. Isaac had remained alive much longer than he had anticipated on the occasion of blessing Jacob. He was nearing the age of 168 at this time of Jacob's return[3] and he still was to live for at least twelve more years, for he died finally at the age of 180 (v. 28). Both Esau and Jacob had a part in burying their father, even as Isaac and Ishmael had in burying Abraham. Apparently Esau came from Edom for the purpose, thus making at least this further meeting between the two brothers an actuality. The burial was made once again in the cave of Machpelah (see Gen. 49:31).

D. Esau's descendants and Edom (Gen. 36:1-43)

1. *Descendants of Esau (36:1-43)*

Because Esau was also the recipient of a divine promise (Gen. 25:23), it was fitting that his posterity receive some notice, as now they do. Esau is directly called Edom (v. 1), since his descendants founded the nation of this name. This was done, however, only after an amalgamation had been made with some earlier inhabitants of the area.

A comparison of the names of Esau's wives, as given in verse 2 and 3 here and in Genesis 26:34 and 28:9 earlier, shows certain differences. The Judith and Basemath of Genesis 26:34 are evidently to be identified with the Aholibamah and Adah here, and the Mahalath of Genesis 28:9 (daughter of Ishmael) with the Bashemath here. Further, the father of Judith in 26:34 is called Beeri, a Hittite, and here Anah, a Hivite. Name changes were not uncommon for the day, and neither was the fact that the same person could have more than one name. As for Judith's father, he evidently was a descendant of both Hittite and Hivite backgrounds.

Five sons of Esau by these wives are listed in verses 4 and 5 and also in 1 Chronicles 1:35. The names of the sons are the same in both listings. The indication of verses 6-8, that Esau took this family and possessions to the land of Seir, need not be taken to mean that he did this only after Jacob had returned from Haran, which would be contrary to the implication of Genesis 32:3 and 33:14, 16. He had likely done this shortly after Jacob had left for Haran, knowing that Isaac's blessing had given the home area to Jacob and that the wealth of both would be too much for them to dwell near each other (see v. 7).

Among the sons and grandsons of Esau, as listed in verses 9-14, the most significant to notice is Amalek, a grandson. It is likely that

---

[3] For evidence of this age, see Keil and Delitzsch, *Commentary on the Pentateuch,* I, p. 320.

he was the father of the later desert tribe, the Amalekites. This was the group that later attacked Israel during their wilderness travel from Egypt to Canaan (Exod. 17:8-14) and whom Samuel instructed Saul to destroy completely as a result (1 Sam. 15:2, 3). It is true that a "country of the Amalekites" is mentioned already in Genesis 14:7, but this could have been only in the sense of this country being where the Amalekites would later roam,

Verses 15-19 give the names of Esau's descendants who became "dukes" (tribal princes) among the Edomites in days to come. There is nothing of significance mentioned regarding any that calls for comment.

2. *Original inhabitants of Seir (Gen. 36:20-30)*

The text now turns from speaking of Esau's family to noting some matters regarding people who lived in Seir before Esau went there. These people are called "sons of Seir the Horite." The term "Horite" now is commonly identified with the well-known people, the Hurrians. A major Hurrian migration is known to have occurred from northern Mesopotamia into southern Canaan during the first half of the second millennium B.C. That migration would have occurred too late to account for these Horites, however, who are mentioned already in Abraham's time (Gen. 14:6). It could be that an earlier migration, in smaller numbers, had transpired. In any event, Horites did live in the region before Esau came, which means that he settled among them. In fact, the Anah and Zibeon, listed in 36:2 as father and grandfather of Esau's wife, Aholibamah, are included in the genealogy given (36:24). Verses 29 and 30 give the names of those who become "dukes" (tribal princes) in the land, serving either before or contemporarily with those from Esau listed earlier.

3. *Kings of Edom (Gen. 36:31-39)*

Now eight kings are listed as ruling in Edom at some time. Since they are called kings of "Edom," rather than kings of "Seir," apparently they all ruled after Esau's descendants had lived long enough in the region to take over leadership and give this name to it. It may be significant, too, that none of these kings is said to have been the son of his predecessor, for this suggests that each was elected to office, and, if so, this probably would have been by the "dukes" listed earlier. These kings, then, would likely have been contemporaneous with at least the later of the "dukes" from Esau.

That they are said to have ruled in Edom "before there reigned any king over the children of Israel" need not be taken to mean that these words were written after the monarchy started in Israel (as critics have often asserted). Moses could well have penned them, knowing that Israel would one day have such kings. God had earlier given specific promise to Jacob that "kings" would come out of his "loins" (Gen. 35:11) and Moses even gave directions as to what kind of a person the Israelites should choose in selecting such rulers (Deut. 17:14-20).

4. *Tribal princes from Esau (Gen. 36:40-43)*

The chapter closes with further names of "dukes" from Esau. Only two of the eleven given correspond to names given earlier (vv. 15-19). The relation between the two lists is best seen to be that this list gives the names of those "dukes" that served in prominent, capital cities of Edom ("after their places," v. 40), and the earlier list only "dukes" in general wherever they served. On this basis, only two of the first list served in or founded such a leading city.

For Further Study

1. In a Bible dictionary or encyclopedia (see bibliography) read articles on: Succoth, Shechem, Hamor, Simeon, Levi, and Edom.
2. Reconstruct the tension that would have existed between Laban and Jacob when Laban caught up with Jacob.
3. In view of all Jacob did in anticipation of his meeting with Esau, reconstruct his thinking and planning in his fear of the encounter.
4. Try to imagine Jacob's experience as he wrestled with the Angel of the Lord.
5. Try to imagine the tension between the people of the region of Shechem and Jacob's family following the slaughter of the Shechemites by Jacob's sons.
6. What do you believe the relation was like between Isaac and Jacob, when they were together again during Isaac's last years?
7. How would you evaluate Esau as a person?

Chapter 12

Joseph (I)

(Genesis 37:1 — 40:23)

Though Jacob continued to live, the stress of the sacred record now turns to the son, Joseph. Joseph was the fourth in the line of the great patriarchs, though he had eleven brothers who also were included in the promised line and became heads of tribes.

A. Joseph and his brothers (Gen. 37:1-36)

1. *Joseph's unpopular position in his home (Gen. 37:1-4)*

The story of Joseph opens when he was seventeen years of age. He had been born six years before Jacob left Haran, meaning that now eleven years had passed since Jacob had returned to Canaan. He is introduced in the role of one tending his father's flocks (along with his brothers). More important, he is shown to have been highly unpopular with them. One reason was that he had brought an unfavorable report to his father concerning their conduct (v. 2); another was that Jacob loved him more than he did the others (v. 3). Jacob showed this love by making Joseph a special coat, because Joseph "was the son of his old age" and had been born to the favored Rachel. The significance of such a coat was that it marked its owner as the son intended by the father as future leader of the family, an honor normally given to the first-born son.

2. *Joseph's unpopular dreams (Gen. 37:5-11)*

Joseph added to his unpopularity by telling both his father and brothers of two dreams given him by God. In one, a sheaf of grain belonging to him remained in an upright position while sheaves belonging to his brothers all bowed before his. In the other, the sun, moon, and eleven stars all made obeisance to him. Both dreams symbolized his own future preeminence over his brothers (which came true later in Egypt), and the second dream showed this pre-eminence to include even his father and deceased mother (in the figure of the sun and moon, the stars representing the brothers). Even Jacob questioned the significance of the second dream, and both dreams served to increase the bitterness of his brothers.

3. *The plot of the brothers against Joseph (Gen. 37:12-27)*

The time was not long before the brothers contrived a plot against Joseph. This occurred on an occasion when Jacob sent Joseph to check on the welfare of the brothers, who were tending the family flocks some distance from home. From Hebron, the family home, Joseph first went north to Shechem to find the brothers. Shechem was well known to the family for this was the place where Jacob had first stopped on returning from Haran. Joseph was told there, however, that the brothers had moved on with their flocks still further north to Dothan (a total distance from Hebron of about sixty-five miles).

Joseph now made his way to Dothan, and the brothers recognized him when he was still some distance from them. They made quick plans to kill him and then throw his body into a pit. Reuben, the eldest, intervened, however, and urged that he be put into the pit alive. Reuben's thought was later to free Joseph so that he might escape the death planned. The brothers were persuaded, and Joseph was put into the pit alive, though they made sure to remove his honored coat first which was such an offense to them. The pit was evidently an abandoned empty cistern, for it is said to have had "no water in it." Its mouth was likely narrow, therefore giving the prisoner no possibility of escape by himself.

After putting Joseph into the cistern, the brothers observed a caravan of traders approaching. The traders are called both Midianites and Ishmaelites (v. 28), suggesting that these two ancestral groups had amalgamated (cf. Judg. 6:2; 8:24). Dothan lay on the overland route between northern Gilead, in Transjordan, and the sea road to Egypt. On seeing the caravan, Judah suggested that the brothers could make a financial profit from Joseph by selling him as a slave to the traders, and the brothers agreed.

4. *Joseph sold into Egypt (Gen. 37:28-36)*

Joseph was sold to the traders for "twenty pieces of silver" (v. 28). Reuben was not present at the time, and, when he found that Joseph had been taken from the cistern, he expressed his great concern and displeasure to the brothers. Being the oldest brother, he no doubt recognized that he would be held primarily responsible by Jacob for any harm done to Joseph.

He may thus have now joined in with a scheme the brothers devised for deceiving Jacob regarding Joseph. They dipped Joseph's fine coat into the blood of a slain goat and then took it to show their father. As they planned, the bloody coat made Jacob think that Joseph had been killed by a wild animal. This caused Jacob to mourn for Joseph many days, and nothing that his sons or "daughters" could do was effective in comforting him. Though the brothers can in no way be excused for this deceit of their father, one is caused to remember that Jacob had also deceived his father many years before, and now was experiencing something of the same remorse that he had brought on Isaac at that time.

Meanwhile Joseph was taken by the traders down to Egypt and sold there as a slave. The shock, suffering, and agony that he experienced can only have been great. He had made a journey of more than sixty-five miles in the interest of his brother's welfare, and the result was that they had first cast him into a cistern and then sold him as a slave. The thought of such complete rejection by them would have been a major emotional blow in itself, but then to be sold as a slave — with all this meant for inevitable suffering and misery — would have been almost more than a person could bear. Certainly at the time Joseph could not have seen how any possible "good" could be involved in such treatment, but still, as later history was to demonstrate, it was. God was working out His plan, though the means seemed impossible to understand at the time.

B. Judah and Tamar (Gen. 38:1-30)

At this crucial point, Joseph's story is interrupted in the sacred account by an unhappy episode in the life of Judah, the fourth son of Leah. It is appropriately inserted here, not only because of chronological sequence, but also because it shows a marked contrast in conduct between Judah and Joseph in somewhat similar situations of temptation. Also, it illustrates one of the reasons for Joseph and later Jacob's whole family going to Egypt at all. Had the family remained in Canaan, all the sons may well have married Canaanite women, as Judah did in this instance, and thus lost the important distinctness necessary for them to become a separate nation as God desired.

1. *Judah marries the daughter of a Canaanite, Shuah (Gen. 38:1-10)*

The time of this episode was probably shortly after the presentation of Joseph's coat to Jacob. Judah left home and went from Hebron down to Adullam in the low country. Adullam was located thirteen miles southwest of Bethlehem and was the place where David later stayed on more than one occasion (see 1 Sam. 22:1; 2 Sam. 23:13). Here Judah took to wife a daughter of a Canaanite named Shuah. They had three children, Er, Onan, and Shelah. Time passed and Judah procured a wife for Er named Tamar. Due to sin on Er's part, God took his life and then Judah instructed Onan to marry Tamar according to the principal of levirate marriage. Onan seems to have been willing to marry Tamar, but then he refused to make the birth of a child by her possible, and God brought about his death also.

2. *Judah and his daughter-in-law Tamar (Gen. 38:11-26)*

Judah then wronged Tamar by sending her to her father's house, saying that she should wait for a husband until the youngest son, Shelah, would be old enough to marry her. Tamar did this, but Judah did not arrange the marriage even though Shelah became old enough to make the marriage possible. As a result Tamar schemed to make Judah himself the father of a child by her. She was wrong in this, but it must be recognized that Judah had first wronged her.

Tamar disguised herself and posed as a prostitute by the road along which she learned Judah would be passing on his way to an occasion of sheep-shearing. The road led to Timnath, about twelve miles northwest of Adullam and the place where Samson would later marry a Philistine girl (see Judg. 14:1-4). Tamar evidently knew that her father-in-law had a sensualistic nature, for her plan worked. Judah saw her and went in to her, thinking she was only a prostitute. She insisted on a pledge of payment from him, which consisted of his "signet," "bracelets," and "staff."

Three months later word came to Judah that Tamar was pregnant. Not knowing that he was the father, and being responsible for her as a member of his family, he ordered her punished. She, however, now proved by the signet, bracelets, and staff that Judah was himself the father, and Judah then admitted his guilt in not having given Shelah to her as a husband. He also rescinded his order for her punishment.

3. *Birth of twins, Pharez and Zerah (Gen. 38:27-30)*

Twin boys were born to Tamar, whom she named Pharez and Zerah. Though Zerah's hand appeared first at the time of birth, he drew back the hand, and Pharez actually entered the world first, and so was the firstborn. Pharez came to be listed as an ancestor of both David and Christ (see Ruth 4:18; Matt. 1:2).

The observation is in order that this sad episode in Judah's life illustrates pointedly the displeasure of God in His chosen people marrying Canaanites. Judah married a Canaanite girl and only trouble resulted from it. First, two of the three sons born to the union died because God was displeased with them. Then Judah was entrapped by his own daughter-in-law in an action that was terribly wrong in itself. And finally he was shockingly embarrassed in finding out that this daughter-in-law, whom he was obliged to punish, could not be punished by him after all, because of sin he had himself committed with her. It seems evident that God wished to tell all Jacob's family that marriages to Canaanites would lead only to unhappy endings.

C. Joseph and Potiphar's wife (Gen. 39:1-23)

In contrast to Judah, Joseph is now presented in the finest light. His experience in Egypt illustrates the truth that, though God's children may be called upon to suffer in this world, they are not forgotten or forsaken by God. Rather, they may expect God's wondrous blessing in His own proper time.

1. *Joseph tempted by Potiphar's wife (Gen. 39:1-13)*

Joseph, though only seventeen when sold as a slave, was evidently a man of remarkable ability. On arrival in Egypt he was sold by the Midianite traders to an important person named Potiphar. He quickly showed his ability in the man's house, for soon Potiphar left "all that he had . . . into Joseph's hand" (v. 4). This degree of responsibility for the young man gave him access to Potiphar's house, and one day the wife of Potiphar proposed to Joseph that they have sinful relations. He rightfully and admirably refused, but she persisted, and on a later day actually forced herself on him to the point where he found it necessary to leave his coat in her clutches to escape from her.

2. *Joseph imprisoned (Gen. 39:14-23)*

Humiliated at Joseph's refusal, the wife presented the coat of

Joseph as evidence that he had attempted to force her. The other servants — no doubt jealous of Joseph anyhow — were quick to believe her, as was also her husband when he returned home. The result was that now Joseph was deprived of his fine position and even cast into prison.

Joseph must be highly commended for his conduct in this experience. Still young in years and far from home restraints, besides having been treated so wrongly by his brothers, it would have been easy for him to give in to this temptation. He did not, however, and provides an excellent example for every young person.

It is to Joseph's further credit that he did not let this crushing incident cause him to be bitter. Being cast into prison, after acting so properly, he might have become discouraged and angry. He did not, however, but once more distinguished himself with fine conduct. As a result, God brought him into favor of the prison keeper, who soon gave Joseph charge of all the other prisoners. Again, Joseph must be highly commended.

D. Interpreting the dreams of the butler and baker (Gen. 40:1-23)

Through these trials of Joseph, God was working out His plan for bringing the young man to the premiership of Egypt, and now in prison another definite step in the plan was effected. Joseph was brought into contact with the butler of Pharaoh, and because he interpreted a dream for the man, Joseph was finally brought to the attention of Pharaoh himself.

1. *Pharaoh's butler and baker have dreams (Gen. 40:1-8)*

While Joseph was in prison, entrusted with his remarkable responsibility over the other prisoners, both a butler and baker of Pharaoh were brought in, having offended their ruler in some way. Thus they came under Joseph's care. One night both dreamed a dream, and the following morning Joseph learned of the fact; he noticed their worried faces and questioned them as to the reason. He asked them to tell him their dreams.

2. *The butler's dream (Gen. 40:9-15)*

The butler told his first. He had seen a vine with three branches bearing blossoms and grapes. Pharaoh's cup was in his hand and he squeezed the juice from the grapes into it and gave the cup to Pharaoh. Inspired of God, Joseph was able to give the interpretation of the dream to the butler. He said the dream meant that within three days the butler would be restored to his position as butler to Pharaoh, and thus be able once again to serve wine to the ruler. Joseph added the request that, when the butler had been restored, he remember Joseph and ask Pharaoh to deliver him from his state as a prisoner; he explained the unjust reason for his being there.

3. *The baker's dream (Gen. 40:16-19)*

Encouraged by this hopeful interpretation of the butler's dream, the baker now told Joseph what he had seen. In his dream, there had been three baskets on his head. Baskets so placed are pictured in Egyptian tomb paintings. In the uppermost of the three were various types of baked foods for the king, but birds came and ate these dainties. Once more, through inspiration, Joseph was able to give the interpretation, only this time it did not portend good for the dreamer.

Joseph said the three baskets symbolized three days, and that at the end of this time Pharaoh would cut off the baker's head and hang his body on a tree wheer the birds would eat his flesh. Just as the butler was pleased with his interpretation, the baker could only have been terribly depressed. It is to Joseph's credit, however, that he told the meanings of the dreams, just as they were, whether pleasant or not. He was completely honest with both men.

4. *The result (Gen. 40:20-23)*

The interpretations of Joseph came true for both men. Within three days the butler was restored to his butlership and the baker was hanged. The impression on the butler, certainly knowing of the baker's bad end just as he did of his good one, could only have been great. Yet in the interest of his self-elevation, he forgot the request of Joseph, who remained in prison. It is so easy to forget the past favors of others when one is absorbed in his own success. Joseph must have been deeply disappointed, for it was not pleasant having to remain in confinement. It was one more trial he had to bear before the exaltation that God had in mind would come.

For Further Study

1. In a Bible dictionary or encyclopedia (see bibliography) read articles on: Joseph, Egypt, caravan, slavery, prison, dreams.

2. Describe the emotional relationship between Joseph and his older brothers.

3. Do you believe Joseph acted wisely in telling his dreams to his brothers? Discuss.

4. Reconstruct Joseph's thinking as he was carried away in the caravan of the traders.

5. Reconstruct the scene as the brothers presented Jacob with Joseph's bloody coat.

6. Why did God put Joseph through such hard testing after his arrival in Egypt?

7. Make a list of the major ways in which Joseph is to be commended for his conduct in these Egyptian trials.

8. Why did God give the dreams to the butler and baker?

Chapter 13

Joseph (II)

(Genesis 41:1 — 45:28)

God often takes His children through a dark night before bringing them to a golden sunrise. He did with Joseph. The young man's night surely had been dark, since being sold as a slave by his brothers, but at last the sunrise came. And what a sunrise it was, as he rose to be exalted to the actual premiership of all Egypt.

A. A dream of Pharaoh results in Joseph's high exaltation (Gen. 41:1-57)

The last step in God's planned road for exalting Joseph was a dream He gave to Pharaoh.

1. *Pharaoh's double dream (Gen. 41:1-8)*

When two more years of prison life had passed for Joseph, God gave Pharaoh a double-type dream. The ruler first saw seven good cows come up from the river (Nile, no doubt). These seven fed contentedly in a meadow near the river. Then seven more cows came up from the river, and these were thin and of poor quality. They came to the first seven and ate them up, thus leaving only themselves as seven poor cows. At this Pharaoh awakened, but once more fell asleep and dreamed. This time he saw seven ears of grain grow full and large on a single stalk. After this he saw seven thin ears, "blasted with the east wind," come after them. Similar to the first dream, the seven thin ears devoured the seven good ones, leaving only the seven poor ones. Then Pharaoh awoke for the second time.

He called immediately for the "wise men" of Egypt to come and tell him what the double dream meant. Both the Mesopotamian and Egyptian sectors of the world had their "wise men," who really were a high rank of priests. They were supposed to be skilled in determining the will of the gods and relaying this to men. Various methods of divination were used, and interpretation of dreams was one. It was therefore natural for Pharaoh to call these men at this time and for them to respond to his call. They had books containing formulas and meanings for giving such interpretations.

In this instance, however, the men either could not or would not give the interpretation. It may be that they just did not want to, since the meaning obviously was not good. For though they could not have given the one correct interpretation, as Joseph soon was to do, the idea of good cows and ears of grain being eaten by poor cows and ears could only have had an unpleasant symbolism in their interpretation as well. Certainly the king was surprised and displeased at their lack of answer to him.

2. *The butler remembers (Gen. 41:9-13)*

The butler, who evidently was nearby, now remembered the event of two years previous. He told Pharaoh of the dreams that he and the baker had seen and how a fellow prisoner of the Hebrews had interpreted the dreams for both. He added, significantly, that both interpretations had worked out as given.

3. *Joseph interprets Pharaoh's dream (Gen. 41:14-32)*

Pharaoh immediately called for this Hebrew, Joseph, to be brought. The indication that Joseph took time "to shave himself" is significant, for it is known that Egyptians did so shave, whereas the people of Canaan and all Asia did not. Properly groomed and attired, Joseph presented himself before the high ruler. When told by Pharaoh that he had heard Joseph could interpret dreams, Joseph significantly and commendably made clear that such interpretations were not of himself but of His God — much as did Daniel years later before Nebuchadnezzar (see Dan. 2:27-30).

Then Pharaoh told him the double dream, speaking first of the two sets of cows and then of the ears of grain. Joseph once more was able to give the interpretation immediately, as in the case of the butler and baker; God apparently gave him the necessary information even as the king told what he had seen. The interpretation was that the seven good cows and ears of grain represented seven years of good crops for Egypt and that the seven bad cows and ears of grain symbolized seven years of poor crops that would follow. The seven poor years would be so bad that all the good of the preceding seven would be consumed by them. The fact that the dream was told doubly meant that the full set of fourteen would begin soon. All this was ominous news for a ruler to hear, and Joseph is to be admired for being willing to give it, when the regular "wise men" had not.

Though Joseph did not mention the matter, the significance of the cows coming up out of the river should not be overlooked. The Nile River was the life line of Egypt. Without it there would not be an Egypt, for rainfall is insufficient to grow crops. The significance was that the Nile would flow in abundance during the first seven years, but then would recede to an inadequate height for the next seven.

4. *Joseph's advice and promotion (Gen. 41:33-46)*

Joseph did more than give this interpretation; he added advice for the king. Pharaoh should select a supervisor to set aside a fifth of the produce during each of the seven plenteous years, so that this could be used during the seven poor years. The advice appealed to Pharaoh and his thinking was that the person who could best fill such a role was the one who had just given the advice. Therefore, he now gave this high position to Joseph, which made the young man virtual premier of the land. In keeping with the honor, Pharaoh put his own ring on Joseph's hand, dressed him in linen, put a gold chain around his neck, and gave him a special chariot, second only to his own for distinction, in which to ride. He further provided him with a wife, Asenath, daughter of Potipherah a priest. Joseph was thirty years old at the time.

Thirteen years thus had passed since Joseph had come as a slave to Egypt. Now he was Egypt's prime minister. Probably no story in the Bible illustrates more pointedly the fact that God controls history. What had seemed like disaster more than once for the young man, God had now turned into the highest honor. Joseph could look back and see how God had been leading even in all the difficult days (see Gen. 45:7, 8), though, at the time, surely those days had been terribly hard and discouraging.

5. *Joseph's administration (Gen. 41:47-57)*

Given sweeping powers by Pharaoh, Joseph set about doing just as he had recommended. During the seven plenteous years he laid food away, until there was so much that its units of measure are said to have been "without number."

During these good years, two sons were born to Joseph and his wife Asenath. The first he named Manasseh (meaning, "causing to forget," a reference no doubt to his earlier experiences) and the second, Ephraim (meaning, "fruitful," as Egypt then was). Later these two boys were to become the heads of two of Israel's tribes.

When the seven years of famine struck, hardship came to all lands around Egypt, but Egypt itself did not suffer because of Joseph's wise preparation. He was able to disperse to the people the food they needed. Learning of this food, people from other lands came as well, and Joseph was able to meet their needs. Certainly Pharaoh was greatly impressed as he saw all of Joseph's interpretation working out exactly as he had given it. No indication is given, however, that he or any other Egyptians turned to believe in the one true God. Satan has a strong hold on men's minds to keep them from believing the truth.

B. Joseph's brothers come to Egypt (Gen. 42:1-38)

At this point, a major development came in God's general plan to bring Jacob's entire family down to Egypt. Joseph's brothers, who had sold him twenty years earlier, now found need to come to Egypt to buy food.

1. *The brothers meet Joseph (Gen. 42:1-28)*

News of the food supply in Egypt came to Jacob's attention, and he sent his sons there to purchase for the family's needs. Canaan had been hit with the drouth, along with Egypt and other lands of the area. Ten of the brothers went, leaving Benjamin with the father. Thus it was that these brothers came to Joseph, and, on seeing him, did not recognize him. Twenty years had brought change to his appearance, of course, but even more, no doubt, they could not possibly think of him being in such a high office. Joseph recognized them, however, as they bowed low before him, even as his dreams of years before had predicted.

He did not let them know he recognized them but instead accused them of being spies in his country. His intent seems to have been to learn concerning matters at his former home, and this the brothers now began to tell him as a way of disproving his accusation. They were all brothers, sons of one father, with one brother having remained with the father and one no longer with them (meaning Joseph). Joseph responded that they could prove their story by sending one of the brothers and bringing the youngest who had stayed with the father. Then he put them all in confinement for three days, apparently to think the matter over. Finally he told them that they could return home, but that one would have to stay until the younger brother was brought.

The thought of having to do this now caused the brothers to speak with each other, not knowing that Joseph could understand them in their native tongue. They called to mind their guilt in connection with Joseph and Reuben asserted that he had warned them at the time. Tears came to Joseph's eyes as he listened. He did not relent, however, but took Simeon as hostage, while permitting the others to return home. When they did, the brothers found that their sacks had been filled with grain and that even the money they had paid for it had been put in the sacks. Discovery of this fact caused them still greater consternation. God has His own way of bringing recompense, and He did so here, working through Joseph. The brothers were made truly to regret the wrong done to him.

2. *Report to Jacob (Gen. 42:29-38)*

One of the most difficult aspects of the whole experience was having to tell Jacob what had happened. The brothers told him that the "lord of the country" of Egypt had spoken "roughly" to them, for which reason they had felt compelled to tell him concerning their family. This had prompted him to insist that their younger brother be brought to prove their story and to keep Simeon with him until they did. They also stated that their money had been returned to them in their sacks of grain. At this Jacob cried out most pathetically, "Joseph is not, and Simeon is not, and you will take Benjamin away: all these things are against me" (v. 36).

Reuben vowed, on the basis of the lives of his own two sons, that he would bring Benjamin back to his father safely, but still Jacob declared that Benjamin could not go to Egypt with them. He was all Jacob had left to remind him of his beloved Rachel and he was not about to lose him.

The question may be asked why Joseph brought this suffering on his brothers and father. The answer in respect to Jacob is that Joseph surely did not intend that he should suffer. He wanted only to see his younger brother, and perhaps did not consider the effect this would have on Jacob. In respect to the brothers, Joseph actually treated them graciously. He had the power of life and death over them, as they stood before him in Egypt. He might have ordered them all killed, in retaliation for what they had done to him. He did not, however. He only wanted to make sure that they remembered their past wrong and experienced appropriate remorse.

This he accomplished. Actually he shows a fine example of one not recompensing "evil for evil" (Rom. 12:17).

C. A second visit by the brothers (Gen. 43:1-45:18)

1. *Preparations for departure (Gen. 43:1-14)*

Though Jacob had meant his words concerning Benjamin, he had no way of providing food for his family without a return visit to Egypt by his sons. Finally he told them to make a second trip, and Judah reminded him of the requirement regarding the younger brother. Judah now took the lead in promising suretyship for the boy, where Reuben had earlier, and finally Jacob relented. He told the brothers to take a "present" for the Egyptian officer and "double money" to make up for the return payment of the first visit. Then he bade them go and take Benjamin, expressing his deep desire that God would give them mercy so that Benjamin might be returned to him safely. Jacob was deeply moved at the time, as were his sons in seeing the anguish of his heart.

2. *The brothers stand before Joseph again (Gen. 43:15-34)*

On seeing his brothers this time, now with Benjamin along, Joseph gave orders that they eat in his own home that noon. This again made the brothers fear, not knowing what this could possibly mean. Their only thought was that it must somehow relate to the fact that their money had been mistakenly returned to them at their first visit, and so they tried to explain how this had happened to the "steward of Joseph's house." The steward tried to reassure them and then even brought Simeon out of his confinement to rejoin them. No indication is given as to the length of time he had been forced to stay in Egypt, while the brothers had been gone, but it had been at least a matter of weeks, for several days are required just to make the journey from Canaan to Egypt.

At noon, when Joseph came to the house, the brothers gave him the "present" they had brought, and he asked them of the health of their father. When Joseph saw Benjamin, he was quite overcome with emotion and had to leave the room. He recovered himself, however, and then gave instructions for the meal to be served. He could not himself eat with the brothers, for it was not considered proper for Egyptians to eat with Hebrews.

When the brothers were seated, they marveled that they were arranged exactly in order, according to age. They could not imagine how this Egyptian could know so much about them. A fivefold portion was given to Benjamin, possibly to test the brothers as to any possible jealousy of Benjamin like that which they had once held for Joseph. They did not show jealousy, however, but actually became "merry with Joseph" in view of his generous treatment of them. Their fears evidently were calmed for a time.

3. *The brothers start home (Gen. 44:1-13)*

Joseph now gave instructions for the grain sacks of the brothers to be filled, with their money once more placed within the sacks. He also directed that his personal "silver cup" be put in the sack belonging to Benjamin. The brothers started for home the following morning, and then Joseph sent his steward after them to catch them and charge them with the theft of the cup. The brothers, not knowing about the cup, strongly denied having taken it and even said that whoever might have taken it should be put to death. When the cup was found in Benjamin's sack, the brothers of course were terribly dismayed. All of them turned and went back to Joseph's city, believing that matters just could not be worse.

4. *The intercession of Judah before Joseph (Gen. 44:14-34)*

On coming to Joseph, the brothers prostrated themselves before him, and then Judah, who had pledged suretyship for Benjamin, began to speak. He first confessed that the brothers had been guilty of sin before God — referring apparently to what they had done to Joseph long years before — and Joseph replied that they needed only to leave Benjamin as his servant in Egypt and the others could go home. This, however, was exactly what Judah did not want, and so he continued to speak, pleading for mercy. He told again of the father and his special love for Benjamin and how the father had not wanted this youngest son to come at all. This led to a mention by him of the father's other son by Benjamin's mother (namely Joseph) and the "mischief" that had befallen him. Therefore, concluded Judah, if the brothers did not bring the one remaining son back to the father, they would bring about the old man's death. He then offered himself in place of Benjamin, to serve Joseph in the boy's stead.

If ever a man interceded for another with full emotional involvement, Judah did here. He who had brazenly suggested the sale of Joseph to the Miadianite caravan years before now was pleading in the greatest humility — and this before the one whom he had sold at that time. How God can bring change and rectification in His own time and way!

5. *Joseph reveals himself to the brothers (Gen. 45:1-15)*

At this pathetic plea, Joseph could restrain himself no longer. His harshness with the brothers had really been play acting, but he could carry this only so far. He now commanded that all persons, other than the brothers, be put out of the room, and then he revealed to them who he was. He was indeed Joseph, whom they had sold into Egypt. He graciously urged them not to grieve over what they had then done to him, for really God had intended the occasion for the purpose of saving life, having now made him a "father to Pharaoh, and lord of all his house" (v. 8). Further, since five years of the famine still remained (making Joseph thirty-nine at this time and Reuben, the oldest brother, forty-five), the brothers should return to Jacob and persuade him to come down and live in Egypt. The entire family could live in the region of Goshen, known for its fertility, and be near him where he could provide for them. Then he embraced Benjamin, his full brother, and even kissed the other brothers, who had treated him so wrongly those many years before.

In this response to the brothers, Joseph showed a great heart. He was able to see beyond the wrong done to him and recognize it as being a part in the all-controlling plan of God. He had the spiritual discernment to recognize that God had used this natural means as a way to accomplish His perfect will. Joseph was a big man, who could forgive and forget. He sets an excellent example.

6. *Jacob is told the good news (Gen. 45:16-28)*

Soon the news that Joseph's brothers had come to Egypt spread throughout the Egyptian palace and even reached the ears of Pharaoh. The monarch was pleased and gave his approval to all that Joseph desired for his family. This is understandable, for Pharaoh owed so much to the wise counsel and work of Joseph. The ruler now urged that the brothers take wagons from Egypt by which to make the move.

At this, the brothers left, this time with contrasting light hearts. They traveled away from Egypt, not only with food, but also with wagons and even changes of clothing. Benjamin had been given, additionally, three hundred pieces of silver. When they told Jacob the news, he could not believe them at first. What they said was just too impossible, but when they insisted and he saw the evidence of the wagons and gifts, he had to be convinced. His spirit now rose to a height unknown for many years, as he said, "It is enough; Joseph my son is yet alive: I will go and see him before I die."

Few days in Jacob's life could have been as happy as this one. Instead of losing also Benjamin, as he had feared, he had now regained Joseph.

For Further Study

1. In a Bible dictionary or encyclopedia (see bibliography) read articles on: Nile River, wise men, famine, Benjamin.
2. Reconstruct Joseph's thoughts and actions as he was told that Pharaoh wanted him to come to interpret a dream for him.
3. Think of his thoughts when Pharaoh actually told him that he would be the premier of the land.
4. In what ways does such exaltation often "spoil" people? Do any of these things seem to have happened with Joseph?
5. How would you characterize Joseph as an administrator?
6. Why did Joseph play act with the brothers as he did?
7. Compare the attitude of the brothers at this time with the occasion when they had sold Joseph.
8. Reconstruct Jacob's thinking as he finally gave permission for Benjamin to go to Egypt with the brothers.
9. Reconstruct his thinking when he heard the news that Joseph was actually alive.

Chapter 14

Joseph (III)

(Genesis 46:1 — 50:26)

The closing section of Genesis tells of Jacob taking his family down into Egypt to live. He was to spend seventeen happy years there, united again with Joseph and having his family complete once more. This move also marked the beginning of a 430-year sojourn of his family in Egypt, while its size grew to that of a nation.

A. Jacob travels to Egypt (Gen. 46:1-34)

1. *Reassurance from God (Gen. 46:1-4)*

Though Jacob had become satisfied in his own heart that he should go to Egypt, he properly felt the need of God's approval for the move. This God gave to Jacob when he arrived in Beersheba. Jacob had been willing to proceed this far, though evidently with some hesitation, for he now stopped to offer sacrifice to God, and this clearly was for the purpose of seeking this approval. God granted it, here in this former home of Abraham and Isaac. He told Jacob that he should indeed go to Egypt and that He would be with him there and would in time bring his family back to Canaan.

2. *The journey to Egypt (Gen. 46:5-27)*

Jacob and his family now continued their journey, using the wagons supplied by Pharaoh. The total group must have spread out for some distance, as the family's flocks and herds moved along beside the long line of wagons.

The text supplies the names of the total group, thus enabling the reader to know exactly how many were included in Jacob's family at the time. The number is given in Genesis 46:27 as seventy, but this includes Joseph and his two sons already in Egypt. In summary, the list includes thirty-two descendants of Leah[1] (vv. 8-15), eleven of Rachel[2] (vv. 19-22), sixteen of Zilpah (vv. 16-18), and seven of Bilhah (vv. 23-25), for a total of sixty-six (v. 26), which, plus Jacob, Joseph, and Joseph's two sons, makes a grand total of seventy.

In Acts 7:14, Stephen refers to the same total group and gives the number as seventy-five, apparently following the Septuagint (Greek) version of both Genesis 46:27 and Exodus 1:5. This seeming discrepancy may be accounted for by understanding the larger figure to include also the five (total) sons and grandsons of Ephraim and Manasseh (see Num. 26:28-37; 1 Chron. 7:14-21).

3. *Arrival in Egypt (Gen. 46:28-34)*

Nearing Egypt, Jacob sent Judah ahead to tell Joseph of their approach. Joseph came immediately to meet his father and family, and the two of them wept as they embraced "a good while." The moment must have been full of emotion for both; they had not seen each other since Joseph had left home so casually some twenty-two years before. Joseph said he could die now, having seen Joseph once again, but actually he was to live for seventeen more years, being 130 here and dying finally at 147 (see Gen. 47:9 and 47:28).

With the greeting having been given, Joseph gave some information and instructions to the family. He would go and tell Pharaoh that the family had come and the family should inform Pharaoh that they were shepherds, so that they would be assigned to Goshen as their area of residence. Apparently Goshen was not populated heavily by Egyptians, though it was fertile and good for grazing livestock. Joseph explained, further, that there was need for a separation between themselves and Egyptians, because Egyptians considered shepherds an abomination.

The observation is in order that, though this necessary separation from Egyptians would have been humiliating to Jacob's family and especially to Joseph as premier, it was all part of God's plan as a way of maintaining Israel's distinctness. If a pure nation was to develop, such distinction was a necessity. Judah's marriage to the Canaanite girl had already shown what would likely have occurred had the family remained in Canaan. Here in Egypt, however, such

---

[1] Verse 15 says 33, but in this figure Jacob evidently is included, and it should be realized that both figures count Dinah, the daughter, and do not include Er and Onan who had died, verse 12.

[2] Verse 22 gives 14, but this includes Joseph and his two sons already in Egypt.

marriages would not be possible. Egypt also would provide good food from the fertile land, and fine cultural advantage as well, for Egypt was then the leading country of the world in standards of civilization.

B. Jacob's family in Egypt (Gen. 47:1-31)

1. *Jacob meets Pharaoh (Gen. 47:1-12)*

Joseph now went to tell Pharaoh that his father and family had arrived, taking five of his brothers with him. When Pharaoh asked them their occupation, as Joseph had indicated he would, they responded as Joseph had directed. Pharaoh then did tell them that they could live in Goshen. Pharaoh also told Joseph that if any of the family was particularly capable with livestock he would like them to care for his own. It may be that his flocks and herds were also kept in Goshen since it was apparently prime land for this purpose.

With these preliminaries taken care of, Joseph brought Jacob himself to see the head monarch. Interestingly, as the two met it was Jacob who extended his blessing on the Egyptian. Pharaoh then asked Jacob how old he was, and Jacob answered 130 years, but he added that he had not yet attained unto the years his fathers had enjoyed — Abraham with 175 and Isaac with 180.

The land of Goshen is rather well identified today with Wadi Tumilat, a valley over thirty miles long, extending from the eastern Nile to Lake Timsah. At first, of course, Jacob's family would have needed only a small part of this extensive stretch, but as time passed and the numbers grew, they would have taken over an increasing amount of it. In this fine region Joseph was able to make sure that the family had the finest of food at all times. It must have been wonderful having the food czar of the country as a member of the family in this continuing time of famine.

2. *Joseph's work in overseeing Egypt (Gen. 47:13-26)*

The text now moves on to tell of the severe hardship that the remainder of Egypt, as well as the world of the general area, experienced during the following five years.

First, the people spent all their money for the food Joseph could supply them. This was placed in the treasury of Pharaoh. When the money ran out, the people traded livestock for food, and when the livestock was gone, they traded their land. In this way, Pharaoh became the owner of the people's money, animals, and finally their land. This made him very wealthy and powerful and all because of Joseph's work in his behalf.

With this ownership of land by the head ruler, a type of feudal system was introduced. The people were issued seed by Pharaoh and then they owed him one-fifth of their produce. Many of the people were forced to move to cities, to make the system work, but apparently even this did not bring a spirit of displeasure, for they simply said of Joseph that he had saved their lives (v. 25).

The measures imposed may seem somewhat harsh, but no doubt they were necessary as a way of saving the country from complete disaster. Hard times call for a tight rein of government, lest rebellion break out. Pharaoh prospered, but no hint is given that Joseph himself took undue gain. The fact that the people praised him shows that they realized the measures were really for their good.

3. *Jacob's last days (Gen. 47:27-31)*

The text now returns to tell further of the contrasting good conditions enjoyed by Jacob and his family. The group increased in both number and possessions. Verses 27 and 28 imply that this was true not only during the five years of famine but also during all of Jacob's continuing seventeen years in Egypt. With the fine land of Goshen in which to live, and with Joseph interested in their welfare particularly, the people had little problem or cause for worry. And, of course, Jacob, seeing all this and having his family complete once more, with Joseph being the honored prime minister of the land, would have been happy indeed.

Finally the time of Jacob's death drew near and he called for Joseph to come. He asked him to swear that he would not bury him in Egypt, but with his fathers back in Canaan. Joseph was happy to do as his father requested, and he placed his hand under Jacob's thigh in the customary sign of the day for an oath (cf. Gen. 24:2). Then Jacob "bowed himself upon the bed's head" (meaning, probably, that he turned over in bed to assume a bowing position) to worship God in glad adoration (v. 31). Hebrews 11:21 refers to this occasion and (following the Septuagint version) speaks of Jacob thus "leaning upon the top of his staff." This additional thought may signify that he employed a staff, which he kept near for the purpose of assisting him in making this movement.

C. Jacob blesses the sons of Joseph (Gen. 48:1-22)

A complete chapter is now devoted to telling of Jacob's blessing on Joseph's two sons, Ephraim and Manasseh. The two were later to become heads of two of Israel's tribes. Joseph did not become a head, but these two sons did. There was need for this, if the total number of tribes was to be twelve, because God had in mind to employ the descendants of Levi as priests for the tribes. This chapter shows that Jacob now formally adopted Ephraim and Manasseh as two more sons, thus to have parallel rights of inheritance along with his direct sons.

1. *Joseph brings his sons before Jacob (Gen. 48:1-11)*

Sometime after the occasion of giving oath, Joseph learned that his father was ill and he came again to see him. This time he brought his two sons, Ephraim and Manasseh (now between eighteen and twenty years old, see Gen. 47:28 and 41:50). Jacob mustered enough strength to raise himself on his bed to speak with the three. He mentioned God's appearance to him at Bethel, when he had seen the dream of the ladder reaching to heaven, and the promise of blessing given at that time. Then he added that these two sons of Joseph were his, even "as Reuben and Simeon," meaning that he was now to adopt them and give them rights parallel with his own sons. He thus was giving honor to Rachel, whom he mentioned at this time, by making three tribes descend from her: Ephraim and Manasseh, as well as Benjamin.

At this point Jacob, who could not see well, asked Joseph to assure him that these two with him were Ephraim and Manasseh, and Joseph did. Then Joseph brought them near to his father, who kissed and embraced them. One cannot help but remember an earlier day when Jacob had come before his own father in deceit to receive a blessing. Perhaps this was why he asked for Joseph's special assurance that these were truly Ephraim and Manasseh.

2. *The blessing bestowed (Gen. 48:12-22)*

The situation was now ready for the actual act of blessing and adoption. Joseph brought the two sons near to the father, with his right hand on Ephraim's head and his left on Manasseh's The reason for doing this was to make it easy for Jacob's right hand (the one of honor) to rest on Manasseh, who was the older of the two.

Jacob, however, crossed his hands so that his right hand came on Ephraim's head and his left on Manasseh's. In this position he pronounced his blessing, asking that God, who had so prospered him, also "bless the lads"; he wanted the name of his fathers to be on them and that they would grow "into a multitude in the midst of the earth" (v. 16).

Now Joseph, seeing the crossed hands of his father, tried to rearrange them, thinking probably that the father had not realized he already had brought the two properly for the oldest to receive the honored position. But Jacob told him that he had crossed his hands intentionally, because the younger brother would become the greater of the two. Manasseh would become great, true enough, but not like Ephraim. Thus he set Ephraim over Manasseh in honor.

Texts found at Nuzi indicate that adoption of this kind was not uncommon in the Middle East of the time. The texts also show that such a blessing, as here bestowed by Jacob (and earlier by Isaac on Jacob), was considered binding in its importance. God also was pleased to use such times of blessing to give revelation concerning the future. Ephraim did become a leading tribe in Israel. In fact, the entire nation of northern Israel came in time to be called frequently by the name of "Ephraim" in the prophetical books (see Isa. 7:2, 5, 9, 17; Hos. 9:3-16; etc.).

Besides the blessing given to the two sons, Jacob also spoke a word to Joseph. He was now granting to Joseph "one portion above" his brothers, a portion of land which he, Jacob, had at some time earlier taken from the "Amorite" (here used generally for "Canaanite") by sword and bow. The occasion when Jacob had taken this portion is probably the same as mentioned in Genesis 33:19, though there he is said to have purchased it. In John 4:5, Jesus, on coming to Jacob's well near Shechem, is said to have come near "to the parcel of ground that Jacob gave to his son Joseph." It was near Shechem, of course, where Jacob bought the property spoken of in Genesis 33:19. In what way he could be said one time to have bought it and another to have taken it by "sword and bow," is not clear. It may be that some force was used, as well as payment in silver. Joseph was buried in the portion in due time (cf. Josh. 24:32).

D. Jacob blesses his own sons (Gen. 49:1-33)

Jacob now called his other sons to him and pronounced "blessing" on them. These blessings were not all of a pleasant kind, however. None of the sons was disinherited, but some were promised much greater benefits than others. Once again, God used this method of "blessing" to give revelation concerning the future of each of the sons and the tribes that would descend from them.

1. *Reuben (Gen. 49:3, 4)*

Jacob addressed the sons of Leah first, taking them in their order of age. Reuben the oldest was the beginning of Jacob's "strength," for he was the firstborn. This meant that by birth this son held the honored position, but Jacob then mentioned a matter which offset this position. Reuben had gone up to his "father's bed," a reference to the time he had sinned with Bilhah (Gen. 35:22). The seriousness of this sin, in the sight of both God and Jacob, is shown by the fact that Reuben's tribe came to play little part in Israel's later history, hardly ever being mentioned, in fact.

2. *Simeon and Levi (Gen. 49:5-7)*

Simeon and Levi, next in order of age, were treated together because they shared in the sin against Hamor and the Shechemites (Gen. 34). Jacob accordingly called them "instruments of cruelty," and predicted that they would be divided "in Jacob" and scattered "in Israel." Levi's descendants came to be divided in the sense that Levites were given cities throughout all the tribes in which to live. Simeon's tribe experienced something similar in being assigned only cities in which to live within the territory allotted to Judah (Josh. 19:1-9).

3. *Judah (Gen. 49:8-12)*

In contrast, Judah received a blessing of distinct honor. His brothers would praise him, and he would be victorious over enemies. In fact, he would assume the position of leadership, forfeited by Reuben, Simeon, and Levi because of their sin, for "the scepter" (of royal authority) would not depart from him "until Shiloh come." Though the word "Shiloh" has been variously interpreted, it almost certainly is a reference to Christ (perhaps as the "Giver of rest," from the Hebrew *shalah* meaning "to have rest"). Thus Judah was promised the kingship, which was realized eventually in David, with the assurance given that this honored status would continue until Christ would come. Christ indeed was born in due time of Judah's tribe, after His human nature, and He will be the final great King of Israel in the millennial age to come.

Then the thought of verses 11 and 12 is that Judah would prosper in his assigned land. Vines would abound, so that animals might be tied to them, and wine from them would be so plentiful that one might wash his garments in it if he chose. The wine would be sufficient, further, to make one's eyes red from overdrinking. Milk too would be abundant, which would make the teeth white.

4. *Zebulun (Gen. 94:13)*

At this point, Jacob had finished with Leah's older sons, but he continued with the two born to her later. Of Zebulun he said that his tribe would live near the sea and be occupied with trading, having a connection in this with "Zidon." Though Zebulun's territory did not come to be assigned directly bordering the Mediterranean, it was near it, and the tribe could easily have benefited from merchandising activity, carried on especially through the port of Sidon to the north. Of this, nothing is known definitely from later history.

5. *Issachar (Gen. 49:14, 15)*

Jacob pictured Issachar as an "ass" (regular beast of burden of the Middle East) lying down under its burden, for it desired rest rather than work; the tribe would thus become "a servant under tribute." The significance is that Issachar, which was assigned land in the fertile Esdraelon Plain, did not choose to seize this land from the native Canaanites, but took the easier way of living wherever its people could find a place. It is evident that they were not in their assigned territory, for instance, in Gideon's day, for his battle with the Midianites was fought in this territory and yet Issacharites are not even mentioned as playing a part in Gideon's army (see Judg. 6:35).

6. *Dan (Gen. 49:16-18)*

The four sons of the two handmaids, Bilhah and Zilpah, were next treated by Jacob though the two of Zilpah, Gad and Asher, were dealt with between the two of Bilhah, Dan and Naphtali.

Jacob used the meaning of Dan's name ("judge") to speak of him, saying that he would judge his people, like the other tribes. He would maintain control over them, because he would be like a "serpent by the way," that is, he would be ready to strike and bring punishing harm on any who deserved it. Later Dan was the tribe which in large part moved from its assigned territory to new land far north. Jacob, however, did not predict this here.

7. *Gad (Gen. 49:19)*

Of Gad, Jacob said only that he would be overcome by a "troop," but that he would retaliate and "overcome at the last." Gad's tribe was assigned land on the east of the Jordan and suffered great hardship by invasion of desert tribes. Its men were valiant fighters for resisting these invasions, however, as implied clearly in both 1 Chronicles 5:18 and 12:8.

8. *Asher (Gen. 49:20)*

Jacob spoke of Asher's future as promising great bounty. The tribe was assigned land along the Mediterranean in the north, and it was fertile for good crops.

9. *Naphtali (Gen. 49:21)*

Jacob described Naphtali as a deer set free to run and also as a person capable in the use of words. The tribe was allotted land next to Asher, north of the Esdraelon Plain. Jacob's reference may be to Naphtali's ability in warfare, being able to maneuver freely like a wild deer. Barak's troops, of whom many were from Naphtali, showed great ability in fighting the Canaanite Sisera (Judg. 4). As for the capable words, reference may be especially to the beautiful song sung at the time by Deborah and Barak (Judg. 5).

10. *Joseph (Gen. 49:22-26)*

Joseph's blessing must be seen as brought to reality principally in his two sons, Ephraim and Manasseh, the two tribal heads. The fruitfulness mentioned by Jacob must be understood mainly in reference to Ephraim, whose descendants became a leading tribe (and whose name meant "fruitful"). The mention of archers shooting at Joseph may refer to Joseph's personal experiences, when he suffered so much and when his "hands were made strong" by God. Joseph's posterity would prosper by the "blessings of heaven" (rainfall), the "blessings of the deep" (spring water), and the "blessings of the breasts and of the womb" (reproduction among men and livestock). Joseph would enjoy the continuation of blessing that Jacob, his father, had experienced before him, and his father, in turn, before him.

11. *Benjamin (Gen. 49:27)*

Jacob spoke of Benjamin as a vicious wolf, devouring prey night and morning. Benjamin became a small tribe, allotted land between the two important tribes, Judah and Ephraim. The tribe developed famous fighters, however, to which reference seems to be made here (see Judg. 20:16, 20-25; 1 Chron. 12:2).

12. *Jacob's directive regarding his burial (Gen. 49:29-33)*

After pronouncing these matters regarding each of the sons, Jacob gave instructions regarding his burial. He had earlier requested Joseph to make sure that he was buried in Canaan (Gen. 47:29-31), but he now spoke to all the sons and gave them more specific directions. He should be placed in the same cave of Machpelah where Abraham, Sarah, Isaac, Rebekah, and Leah now reposed. When these words had been spoken, the old man laid back in bed and "yielded up his spirit" in death.

E. Burial of Jacob and the death of Joseph (Gen. 50:1-26)

1. *Burial of Jacob (Gen. 50:1-14)*

Joseph seems to have taken immediate charge of arrangements when his father died. He first gave orders for the embalming of his father. The art of embalming had been developed in Egypt to a high degree of sophistication by this time. The process occupied forty days and the mourning for Jacob, even among the Egyptians, lasted seventy days, no doubt out of respect for Joseph.

When these matters had been cared for, Joseph explained to Pharaoh that his father had requested burial in Canaan, and Pharaoh gave his permission for Joseph to comply. He even sent Egyptian servants along to help, as well as "elders" of Egypt. The procession must have been long that moved out of Egypt, headed for Canaan. It included all these Egyptians besides, of course, the Israelites, who left only their children and animals in Egypt, with even "chariots and horsemen" in attendance. A stop of seven days, perhaps to rest, was made at "the threshing-floor of Atad" (unknown) which was beyond the Jordan (the east side). This notice of location means that a long route had been taken, going around the southern end of the Dead Sea, perhaps to avoid possible antagonistic Canaanite peoples of the south.

Seeing this immense funeral procession, local Canaanites called the place of this stop "Abel-mizraim," meaning, "meadow of the Egyptians." Because the Semitic word for "meadow" is close in pronounciation to the word for "mourning," it is likely that a play on words was intended, so that an element of both meanings was in mind. People were amazed at seeing an Egyptian funeral procession so far from Egypt.

Finally the cave of Machpelah was reached, and there the body of Jacob was laid to rest, thus making a total of six people buried there. Today, in the mosque of Macpelah at Hebron, monuments to all six are to be seen. With the burial completed, the procession returned to Egypt, no doubt having taken many days for the complete journey.

2. *Joseph's brothers now fear him (Gen. 50:15-21)*

With Jacob dead, the brothers now feared that Joseph might bring vengeance on them because of their early treatment of him. Accordingly, they sent word to him that Jacob had expressly instructed that he forgive them. Whether Jacob had actually done this or not is not made clear. Joseph had been present at the final time of blessing by Jacob and so would have heard if such instructions had been given then. The brothers may simply have contrived the story in the interest of their own safety. Whatever the case, Joseph was deeply grieved that they should even think that he might harm them. He did not impose any penalty on them, however, but only assured them that he would continue to care for them as before. Joseph surely provides a fine example of a true forgiving spirit.

3. *Joseph's last days (Gen. 50:22-26)*

Joseph lived to an age of 110, which means that his death occurred fifty-four years after that of Jacob. During this time he was able to see Ephraim and Manasseh's children and grandchildren. Before his death, he assured the Israelite family that God would indeed bring them back to Canaan in due time, and he made them take an oath that they would take his body with them when that happened. The result was that, when he died, he was embalmed and placed in a "coffin" (mummy-case) in Egypt, where his body remained until the time of the Exodus many years later. He was not taken back to Canaan immediately, then, like Jacob. His body was taken along at the time of the Exodus (Exod. 13:19) and on reaching Canaan was buried in Shechem (Josh. 24:32). His tomb can still be seen there today, not far from Jacob's well.

For Further Study

1. In a Bible dictionary or encyclopedia (see bibliography) read articles on: Pharaoh, Goshen, oath, embalming, Machpelah.

2. Picture in your mind the moment of greeting between Joseph and his father.

3. Why was it necessary for Jacob's family to remain distinct from their neighbors?

4. Make a list of the things that would have made Jacob's last seventeen years happy.

5. Do you think Joseph's measures with the Egyptian people, during the famine, were too harsh? Discuss.

6. Why did Jacob wish to adopt Joseph's sons as his own?

7. How important were "blessings" as bestowed by fathers on their sons?

8. Why did both Jacob and Joseph want to be buried in Canaan and not Egypt?

9. Picture the long funeral procession that took Jacob's body from Egypt to Canaan.

Bibliography

Bible Dictionaries and Encyclopedias

The following reference works are useful for reading articles as suggested at the close of each chapter.

Douglas, J. D., ed. *The New Bible Dictionary*. Grand Rapids: Wm. B. Eerdmans Publishing Co., 1962.

Orr, James, ed. *The International Standard Bible Encyclopedia,* 5 vols. Grand Rapids: Wm. B. Eerdmans Publishing Co., 1939.

Tenney, Merrill C., ed. *The Zondervan Pictorial Bible Dictionary,* rev. ed. Grand Rapids: Zondervan Publishing House, 1967.

Tenney, Merrill C., ed. *The Zondervan Pictorial Bible Encyclopedia,* 5 vols. Grand Rapids: Zondervan Publishing House, 1975.

Unger, Merrill F., ed. *Unger's Bible Dictionary*. Chicago: Moody Press, 1957.

Commentaries on Genesis

The following commentaries on Genesis are among the more useful.

Barnhouse, Donald G. *Genesis*. Grand Rapids: Zondervan Publishing House, 1973.

Calvin, John. *Commentaries on the First Book of Moses Called Genesis,* 2 vols. Grand Rapids: Wm. B. Eerdmans Publishing Co., 1948.

Candlish, Robert S. *Commentary on Genesis,* 2 vols. Grand Rapids: Zondervan Publishing House, n.d. Original edition by Adam and Charles Black of Edinburgh, 1868.

Davis, John J. *Paradise to Prison*. Grand Rapids: Baker Book House, 1975.

Jamieson, Robert. *Genesis — Deuteronomy* in *A Commentary on the Old and New Testaments,* vol. I. Grand Rapids: Wm. B. Eerdmans Publishing Co., 1945.

Keil, C. F. and Delitzsch, F. *The Pentateuch,* 3 vols. in *Biblical*

Commentary on the Old Testament. Grand Rapids: Wm. B. Eerdmans Publishing Co., 1949.

Lange, John P. *Genesis, or the First Book of Moses* in *A Commentary on the Holy Scriptures*. New York: Charles Scribner's Sons, 1915.

Leupold, H. C. *Exposition of Genesis*. Columbus: The Wartburg Press, 1942.

Murphy, J. G. *Commentary on the Book of Genesis*. Andover: Warren F. Draper, 1866.

Smith, R. Payne. *Genesis* in *Genesis to Numbers,* vol. I in *A Bible Commentary for English Readers,* ed. by C. J. Ellicott. New York: E. P. Dutton & Co., n.d.

Stigers, Harold. *A Commentary on Genesis*. Grand Rapids: Zondervan Publishing House, 1975.